2nd Edition, Revised & Expanded

LinkedIn Makeover

Professional Secrets to a POWERFUL LinkedIn® Profile

Donna Serdula

Dedication

The first edition of this book was dedicated to my father. He was the one who pressed me to write it and bugged me until I finished it. He died just two weeks after receiving his copy. The dedication surprised him and he loved it. This second edition is dedicated to his memory. Here you go, Daddy! I love you and miss you so very much.

Table of Contents

Introduction

I signed up for the relatively new business social networking site, LinkedIn® in 2005, or was it 2006? Who remembers? It certainly didn't seem like a momentous occasion at the time. Not only was it not memorable, I had no idea that LinkedIn® would become a huge part of my business life and directly help me find prospects and clients. Perhaps had I known then what I know now, I might have attempted to create a more dynamic profile. Instead, I spent about 15 minutes copying and pasting my out of date resume into most of the profile fields.

Once finished, I leaned back and wondered when opportunity would start knocking. LinkedIn® had promised unlimited opportunity and the ability to connect to a trusted network of contacts. Well, nothing happened. Opportunities did not abound and not only did LinkedIn® make no sense to me, it seemed like a huge waste of time.

Fast forward a few months... I was working as an Account Executive for a software company. My days were spent filling my sales funnel through cold calling and trying to close business. My view of LinkedIn® changed one late afternoon when I connected with a prospect after making my umpteenth phone call of the day. We had a great conversation and I was able to schedule a meeting. I remember excitedly hanging up the phone and immediately Googling my new prospect's name. I wanted to learn as much about this person as possible.

As soon as I hit the search button, a feeling of dread came over me. Somehow, I just knew at this exact moment, my prospect was searching my name on Google, too!

What in the world would he find?

I immediately charted a new course of action and Googled MY name. My LinkedIn® profile was the only pertinent result in the small handful of sites that were returned. I opened my LinkedIn® profile and looked at it through the eyes of my potential client.

How would he react to it? My profile was half-filled out. Is my prospect thinking I do not finish things I start? My profile was clearly plagiarized from my resume. Is he thinking I lack creativity and energy? I never bothered getting a single recommendation from a client. Is he assuming I do not have any satisfied customers? I did not join any groups or list any organizations. Does he consider me a novice and not an expert in my field?

A sinking feeling came over me and I realized that my LinkedIn® profile did not portray me as a top notch professional. My LinkedIn® profile did not sell my skills or show any differentiation between me and the millions of other LinkedIn® users out there. My profile basically said, "This lady doesn't have anything that sets her apart from the crowd."

At that moment I realized this issue needed to be rectified. My LinkedIn® profile had to stand out from the crowd and sell me as a dynamic sales professional who naturally attracts clients and opportunities. Not knowing what made a profile great, I decided to research the best LinkedIn® profiles to see what made them shine. I read tons of blog entries that explained profile optimization strategies and I began to experiment with my own profile. Soon, I was writing and rewriting my LinkedIn® profile until I crafted something that was compelling to my readers, showcased my skills, and marketed me as an expert in my field.

Soon after performing my LinkedIn® makeover, I started to notice that my meetings with prospects began going smoother. It was like they already knew me. Prior to the makeover, I had to work hard to build their confidence. After the makeover, my profile gave my prospects the information they needed to start forming a rapport with me before I even walked through the door. Additionally, recruiters started calling. Old colleagues and schoolmates began contacting me to reconnect.

LinkedIn® suddenly started to make sense.

As it turns out, in order to find success on LinkedIn®, you need to actually use it. As my LinkedIn® inbox began filling with requests to connect, I could not help but use it even more. I quickly realized that I could get past the gatekeeper by sending InMails straight to decision-makers. It was easy to stay in touch with people I met at industry events simply by requesting to connect with them on LinkedIn® afterwards. Before I knew it, I was throwing away business cards and keeping my rolodex of contacts on LinkedIn®.

I began giving and requesting recommendations from colleagues and clients. I joined LinkedIn® Groups and started discussions that showcased my expertise.

By using LinkedIn®, I became a sought after sales professional with a rapidly growing customer base.

In 2009, I decided it was time to embark upon a dream and start my own business. I wanted to share my social media and social networking experiences with others by showing them how this new media could help grow their businesses and forge strong relationships with prospects and customers.

It did not take long before I found myself receiving requests to optimize my clients' LinkedIn® profiles. Eventually I decided to spin this portion of my business off onto its own Website, LinkedIn-Makeover.com.

Since I started LinkedIn-Makeover.com, I have written thousands of LinkedIn® profiles. This book is born from my original research and from the knowledge and skills I developed writing LinkedIn® profiles for executives, entrepreneurs, television personalities, government officials, sales professionals, consultants, job seekers, and thousands of other professionals from all over the world.

I've worked with people from Australia, New Zealand, Russia, France, Netherlands, Saudi Arabia, India, Canada, and so many other places. What really surprised me is despite the cultural differences and disparate backgrounds, my clients have one thing in common. They recognize the power of the Internet and how important it is to use this technology to shape their own digital identity. They realize that in order to succeed, they need to take control of their Internet presence and truly present themselves in a way that inspires, impresses, and builds confidence in their abilities, products, and services. They choose to use their LinkedIn® profile as a tool to lend credence to their professional brand.

Why LinkedIn®?

LinkedIn® is the most popular professional social networking site out there today. Facebook may have over a billion members but LinkedIn® has a global audience of over 200 million professionals and business people. People use LinkedIn®, not for sharing pictures of kittens, but for business networking.

LinkedIn® has become an important tool for companies and professionals. Companies use LinkedIn® to post jobs and research potential employees, vendors, and partners. Business professionals use LinkedIn® to find products, services, and potential alliances.

Clearly, LinkedIn® is the ultimate database for professionals. Whether you are looking to get hired or network with industry leaders or promote yourself, LinkedIn® is the place to be.

So why aren't you there with bells on? You'd never show up to an in-person networking event or business meeting with jeans and a ripped t-shirt. Your LinkedIn® profile is your online business suit and it should make you look your best.

Personal branding is imperative in this Google world. People are researching you and forming an opinion based upon what they find. You are who you say you are and you have full control over people's perception of you. By having a strong, optimized LinkedIn® profile, you are branding yourself as a high performing professional. Your LinkedIn® profile is the place to tout your accomplishments and showcase endorsements and recommendations. If you don't highlight your accomplishments, I can assure you no one else will.

This book will show you how to easily create a profile that will get you noticed, enhance your reputation and prove you are an expert in your field. Over the course of this book, I will reveal my secrets to creating a powerful LinkedIn® profile in a step by step, easy to understand manner. Each chapter is designed to help you strategically build an online presence that is impressive and gets you closer to your desired future.

I am going to assume you already have a profile but if you don't, no worries. Just register: http://www.LinkedIn.com

Getting Started

Before we dive into optimizing your LinkedIn® profile, there are a few things you need to do first. Almost all my clients ask me one question before we begin, "How can I make sure my contacts don't see the changes I make to my LinkedIn® profile?"

Activity Settings

When you make changes to your profile, an update is sent out alerting your network. These updates are a great way to stay top of the mind aware with your LinkedIn® connections. In fact, I frequently tell clients to make edits to their profile at least once a month so they are assured placement in the weekly LinkedIn® update email that goes out to their connections.

LinkedIn® updates are sent out to your connections if you:

- Upload or edit your profile picture
- Update your profile's headline
- Add a new current job position
- Add a new current school
- Add a new link to a Website
- Recommend someone
- Add a connection
- Follow a LinkedIn® Company page
- Follow news
- Join a LinkedIn® Group

Regardless of the benefits, there are times when you don't want people to know you are making changes. Perhaps you are updating your LinkedIn® profile in the quest to find a new job. It's probably best your employer isn't notified of such a change.

Luckily, LinkedIn® provides the ability to turn off your Activity broadcasts so you can make changes to your LinkedIn® profile without alerting your connections.

Turning off LinkedIn® Update Alerts

1. Open LinkedIn® in your favorite browser.
2. Hover your mouse over your image in the upper right hand corner of your screen. An expanded menu appears.
3. Click Privacy & Settings.
4. Under Privacy Controls within the Profile section, click Turn on/off your activity broadcasts.
5. Remove the checkmark from: Let people know when you change your profile, make recommendations, or follow companies.

When your profile is optimized, I highly suggest turning the activity updates back on. All you need to do is follow those steps and put the checkmark back in place.

Benchmarking for Success

Now that you have cloaked your LinkedIn® profile edits, it's time to benchmark. You see, in order to determine success, you need to know where you started.

How many views are you currently getting to your LinkedIn® profile? How many times do you show up in LinkedIn®'s search results per day? How many 1st degree connections do you have? How strong is your LinkedIn® network?

Profile Views & Search Results

LinkedIn® provides statistics that show you how well your profile is performing. You can find these stats on your LinkedIn® home page.

Who's Viewed Your Profile?

1.   Click Home on LinkedIn's top navigation bar.
2.   On the right hand side of the screen, look for the module
        with the title: Who's Viewed My Profile?

The Who's Viewed My Profile module shows how many people have viewed your profile in the past day, 3 days, 30 days or 90 days.

This is the number of people who actually clicked on your profile to view it. When you click on the See more link, you are taken to the Profile Stats page where you can see how many times your profile appeared in LinkedIn® search results.

Please enter these statistics on the Benchmarking Workbook located in a couple pages. Don't worry if the stats are good or bad. I promise you that before you finish optimizing your profile, you will see improved results.

LinkedIn® Network Stats

Now it's time to record the number of people currently populating your LinkedIn® network.

How Many People Are In Your Network?

1.   Click Home on LinkedIn®'s top navigation bar.
2.   On the right hand side of the screen, look for the module
        with the title: Your LinkedIn® Network.

The LinkedIn® Network module shows the number of 1st degree connections within your LinkedIn® network. 1st degree connections are people you are directly connected to within LinkedIn®. They may be people you invited to connect or people who invited you to connect. This box also states how many people are in your entire LinkedIn® network. You see, your LinkedIn® network is comprised of people who are connected to you within three degrees. Don't worry too much about what this means just yet, we will cover this in a later chapter.

You will revisit these statistics at the end of the book. In order to know the optimization is working, you must know exactly how well your profile was performing before you started.

Benchmarking Worksheet - BEFORE

Who's Viewed Your Profile?

Your profile has been viewed by:

_____ people in the past _____ day(s).

Search Results

How many times you appeared in LinkedIn Search: _____

LinkedIn® Network Stats

_____ Connections link you to _____ professionals.

_____ New people in your network since _____.

Should I Upgrade?

There are two types of accounts on LinkedIn®, the free and the paid versions. Which one is right for you?

The free account is a good starting point for most users. It allows you to do almost everything that the paid version does, only in limited number and with limited visibility. For example, a free account only shows the first 100 results of a LinkedIn® search; whereas a paid account provides anywhere from 3 to 10 times that amount of results.

There are four different types of paid accounts ranging from $24.95 a month to $499.95 a month. The higher the price, the more you can do within LinkedIn®.

Although the free account is a good starting point, I do advocate upgrading. LinkedIn® provides a very cheap introductory plan called Personal Plus. It is only $7.95 a month, if paid annually.

Premium plan users get a badge on their profile that identifies them as paid users. This badge is a great way to signal that you are a serious user and not a cheapskate. Besides, it shows your support for a wonderful company.

The premium plans have many selling points that make the monthly fee reasonable. One of the more awesome abilities you gain from upgrading is the ability to see who has viewed your LinkedIn® profile. This is great information and we will talk more about it at the end of this book.

My recommendation for you right now is to start with the basic account. I'll walk you through the steps of upgrading to the Personal Plus plan in a few chapters.

Time to Jump into LinkedIn®

Maria, from *The Sound of Music*, sang, "Let's start at the very beginning; it's a very good place to start!" But you are a rebel and you will start at the end because when it comes to LinkedIn®, the easy stuff is at the bottom of your profile. So what are you waiting for? Let's begin at the end.

Editing Your LinkedIn® Profile

1.   Login to LinkedIn®.
2.   Click Profile > Edit Profile on LinkedIn®'s top navigation bar.
3.   Scroll to the very bottom of the page.

Following, Groups, and Connections is where you will start. It's the last section of your profile and our Chapter 14.

14

The End

Following News & Companies
Connections ★ Groups

Following News & Companies

When you first log in to LinkedIn®, you land on their home page. Their home page contains a number of interesting items. This is where you post status updates that will potentially be seen by your connections. It's also where you read status updates made by your connections. Think of this newsfeed as your own customized newspaper, curated by all of your direct, 1st degree LinkedIn® connections. You are not limited to just status updates from connections. You can also subscribe to news items, company updates and original content from influencers. In order to tap into this stream of information, all you have to do is follow news items, companies, and influencers that interest you.

By following companies and influencers, you get their status updates on your home page and you show your interest and allegiance to them on your LinkedIn® profile.

At the very bottom of your LinkedIn® profile is the Following section and within the section, logos of the companies and news you followed are displayed. In order to populate this section, you must follow some companies and news sources.

You can follow as many as 1,000 companies and an unlimited number of news sources or industries.

Following a Company

1.   Click in the search box located at the top of the LinkedIn® screen and type the name of a company you'd like to follow on LinkedIn®.
2.   Click the magnifying glass icon or the enter key on your keyboard to execute the search.
3.   Select the company name from the results page. The company's LinkedIn® Company page will open.

4.   Click the Follow button on the upper right hand side of the company's Overview page. The button will change to Following.

Companies you follow are displayed on your profile. My recommendation is to follow at least 5 companies to show you are using LinkedIn® as a way to get information. Not sure what companies to follow? No worries, here are some ideas to get you started:

- Your current company
- The companies you worked in the past
- Your dream company
- Companies that are current or prospective customers
- The companies where your friends and family members work

If you go overboard and follow more companies than you can keep up with, you can stop following a company and its updates.

How to Stop Following a Company

1.   Click Profile > Edit Profile on LinkedIn®'s top navigation bar.
2.   Scroll down to the Following section and click the edit icon.
3.   Scroll down to Companies.
4.   Hover over the word, Following that appears under the logo. It will momentarily change to Unfollow. Once you click it, it will update to +Follow.

Following News

Also on LinkedIn®'s home page is a summary of news items found on LinkedIn® Today. LinkedIn® Today is content curated by LinkedIn®. These are the top business stories of the day. By following a news source or industry on LinkedIn® Today, you are customizing the content based upon your preferences.

How to Follow News Items

1. Click Interests > Influencers on LinkedIn®'s top navigation bar.
2. Click the All Channels tab.
3. Click the News items you are interested in following.

Following Influencers

Not only does LinkedIn® provide you with curated content from around the Web, you can also tap into original content by thought leaders. These influencers share their knowledge and insights through original articles found exclusively on LinkedIn®.

How to Follow an Influencer

1. Click Interests > Influencers on LinkedIn®'s top navigation bar.
2. Click the All Influencers tab.
3. Click the Influencer you are interested in following and when their overview page opens, click the Follow button on the upper right corner.

Connections

The power of LinkedIn® is that it links people together. LinkedIn® makes invisible connections between people *visible*.

Understanding Your LinkedIn® Network

LinkedIn® uses the terms 1st, 2nd, and 3rd degree connections to define your relationships with your network of connections. A 1st degree connection is someone you have added to your network or they have added you to their network. 1st degree connections are directly connected to you. People within your 1st degree network can message you. They can also recommend, endorse and suggest profile updates. When you post a status update, it's the people in your 1st degree network that see and comment on it.

A 2nd degree connection is a person connected to your 1st degree connection but not directly connected to you. A 3rd degree connection is someone who is connected to a 2nd degree connection. If a person is considered outside your network, you do not share any connections within 3 degrees of that person.

Your LinkedIn® Network Visualized

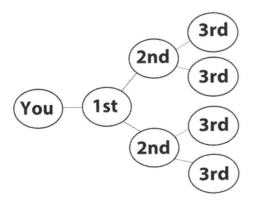

By connecting with as many people as you can, you are increasing your network because it is not just who you know directly but who your connections know and who their connections know

You can see how people are connected to you by viewing their LinkedIn® profile. On the right hand side of their profile, there is a graphic that shows your shared connections.

Connections are critical to your success on LinkedIn®. When you search LinkedIn® for people or companies, the results are comprised of people within your LinkedIn® network who meet your search criteria. When people search for you or someone like you, you will appear in their search results as long as you reside within their LinkedIn® network.

The more people you have in your network, the higher you rank in LinkedIn® search and the more often you will get found.

Should I Connect with People I Don't Know?

Your LinkedIn® network is the most valuable part of LinkedIn® and the key to truly leveraging the system. There are two competing philosophies in the LinkedIn® world. There are some people who believe you should only connect with people you know and trust. This is exactly what LinkedIn® wants you to do and they even state so in their User Agreement. When you connect to only people you know and trust, your LinkedIn® network is naturally smaller; however, because you know everyone personally, you can confidently recommend and introduce people without worry. The other school of thought bucks legality and believes that connecting is a good thing. Why limit yourself to only people you know and trust? When you go to a networking event, you don't stay amongst the people you know and trust. Instead you branch out, working the room to meet new people. Why should it be different on LinkedIn?

People who follow this open networking philosophy are known as LIONS.

LinkedIn® Open Networkers

A LION or LinkedIn® Open Networker is a LinkedIn® user who understands the power of having a large LinkedIn® network. LIONs will connect with almost anyone on LinkedIn® regardless of whether they know, trust, or even respect the person.

Once I became a LION and my LinkedIn® network grew, my profile appeared more often in search results and the views to my profile skyrocketed. Since there were so many people in my LinkedIn® network, more people saw my status updates and my profile. Opportunities rushed at me and my business grew.

There are rules to being a LION. It's not as simple as connecting with anyone and their brother. Remember how I said that LinkedIn® only wants you to connect with people you know and trust? LinkedIn® polices this policy by providing different options for a person to either accept or reject your invitation to connect. When you send out an invitation, the recipient has a few options:

1.   They can accept your request.
2.   They can ignore your request.
3.   They can report your request as SPAM.

By accepting your request they are accepting you into their network. When this happens everything is hunky dory. By choosing Ignore, the recipient archives your request. If the recipient does nothing more at this point, everything remains hunky dory. However, two more options will appear:

- I Don't Know
- Report as SPAM

By choosing I Don't Know or Report as Spam, the recipient of your invite is citing you as an abusive LinkedIn® user. If you receive five invites marked as I Don't Know, your LinkedIn® account is restricted. When this happens, each time you try to add a connection as a friend, you must enter their email address. This is a major inconvenience to say the least.

If you continue to get cited as an abusive LinkedIn® user, LinkedIn® will terminate your account. Say goodbye to your profile, connections, inbox and groups.

Rather than aim low and wide, you must make sure you only invite people who will not click Report as SPAM or I Don't Know. By connecting with people who are LinkedIn® Open Networkers, you can rest assured you are safe from the dreaded SPAM/IDK label.

Accepting someone into your LinkedIn® network is not the same thing as endorsing them as an upstanding human being. Your LinkedIn® network is simply a network of connections. You may not particularly like someone as a person but if they have a large network, it would behoove you to connect with them anyway. Remember, it's not who you know directly, it's who your connections know.

Right now, you might be thinking, "What if my competitor wants to connect with me? He can steal my connections!"

Remember what Michael Corleone said in *The Godfather Part II*?

"My father taught me many things here — he taught me — keep your friends close but your enemies closer."

Connecting with competitors isn't such a bad thing. It's not just your network that is opening up. You are getting access to their network. And by having a large network, there is no way that your competitor can cherry pick your clients. Besides, by connecting, you can keep your eyes on your competitor by watching their status updates and recommendations.

It's important to realize the implications the different connecting philosophies offer. You must decide what makes the most sense for your LinkedIn® goals. You may decide that you will strive for a strong network consisting of people you know and trust while conservatively connecting with some LIONs who provide in roads to your target audience. You have control over your network and you choose what makes the most sense for you.

Invitation Limits

Everyone has limits… including LinkedIn®. LinkedIn® users can send up to 3,000 invitations. Once that limit is reached, you have to ask LinkedIn® to provide you with more. As long as you play nicely in their sandbox, LinkedIn® will provide you with another 500 invitations. Here it is in their own words:

> *LinkedIn® initially allows all users to send up to 3000 invitations. This limit is an automatic method to prevent accidental abuse and protect both senders and recipients. The limit is in place only to prevent abuse, not to block invitations sent by careful inviters. LinkedIn® encourages all users to connect to their trusted professional contacts and to others who welcome connections with new contacts. Users who limit their invitations to these two groups have high invitation acceptance rates and LinkedIn® will usually raise the limit for such inviters.*

> *http://www.linkedin.com/static?key=pop/pop_more_invitation_limits*

The smart strategy is to get people to invite you, that way you don't use up your invitations.

Changing Who Can See Your Connections

When viewing a 2nd or 3rd degree LinkedIn® profile, you can see how that person is connected to you through your shared connections. When viewing a 1st degree LinkedIn® profile, you can potentially view their entire list of 1st degree connections.

Some people do not want to share their list of connections even with their 1st degree network. I had a client who spent 30 years creating a strong network of professional connections. When she joined LinkedIn®, she made sure to connect with this strong network. It was an amazing compilation of leaders, high performers, VIPs and movers & shakers. She immediately realized that by connecting with the wrong person, they could easily take advantage of the network she spent 30 years building. Luckily, LinkedIn® allows the ability to opt out of sharing your connections list with your 1st degree connections.

Turning off Your Connections List

1.	Click Profile > Edit Profile on LinkedIn®'s top navigation bar.
2.	Scroll down to the Connections section.
3.	Click the Customize Visibility link:

Select who can see your connections. Note: People will always be able to see shared connections.

 Your connections

☐	Only you

The recommended setting is to make your connections list visible. If you would prefer to keep your list away from prying eyes, select Only You from the drop list.

Are there repercussions to disabling your connection's list? The whole point of LinkedIn® is to connect with people. When you disable your connection's list, you are closing your network off to people. Although there are no limitations when you close off your connections, some people may take issue especially if you browse their 1st degree network. You decide the best choice for you; either option is entirely acceptable.

Regardless of whether you decide to disable or enable your connections list, your connections will always be able to see shared connections.

Groups

The Groups section is where you show the world your involvement in your industry and community. Group logos appear on your profile after joining.

Groups allow you to forge new business relationships with like-minded professionals. You can post news, participate in discussions, and network. It is a great way to add value and learn from others.

Here is another fantastic thing about LinkedIn® Groups: they allow you to expand your LinkedIn® network. People in the same LinkedIn® Groups as you are considered part of your LinkedIn® network even if they aren't 1st, 2nd, or 3rd degree connections.

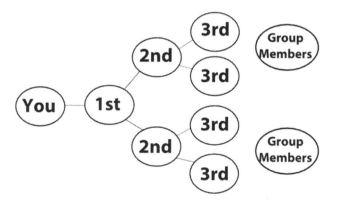

The most awesome part of group membership is that you can make direct contact with a fellow LinkedIn® Group member without an introduction or InMail.

Let's say there is a person you've been wanting to message on LinkedIn® but you aren't directly connected to them. All you have to do is join a LinkedIn® Group they belong to and suddenly you can send them a message within LinkedIn®. How do you know which groups they belong to? Just visit their

LinkedIn® profile. You can join up to 50 LinkedIn® Groups. I suggest joining all 50 groups so you can expand your network as far as possible.

Joining Groups

1. Click Interests > Groups on LinkedIn®'s top navigation bar.
2. On the right hand side of the page, LinkedIn® suggests groups you may like. Click More to see additional groups.
3. On the left hand side of the page, search for a specific group name or search for keywords that will lead you to groups who share that subject.
4. The next page will show you all the groups that match your criteria. Review the groups and click Join.

The LinkedIn® Groups you join should contain your customers and not your competitors. This may sound like an obvious piece of advice but I have found people flock to groups that are directly related to their job. If you are an Insurance Broker, you may find yourself tempted to join groups on insurance but you are only going to find other Insurance Brokers. Your customers probably belong to LinkedIn® Groups for business owners and Human Resource professionals. Figure out what LinkedIn® Groups attract your target audience and join those groups.

The other thing to consider when joining LinkedIn® Groups is the number of members within the group. Your network grows by the number of people in the group so choose LinkedIn® Groups with the most members. The bigger your network, the more people you can see and the more people who can see you. I am not going to just yet tell you how to interact in LinkedIn® Groups. Right now I simply want you to concentrate on joining groups with large numbers of your target audience. We'll get into interacting in groups later.

13

Recommendations

Giving & Receiving Recommendations
The Perfect Recommendation

Recommendations

Recommendations are testimonials that appear on your profile, showing your reader you are trusted and admired within your network. Unfortunately, in order to get recommendations on your profile, you must rely on other people to provide them.

Recommendations allow other LinkedIn® users to provide testimonials about your value and abilities. Perhaps you are being considered for a new job? Recommendations from people in high places will set you apart from other job applicants. If you are using your profile for branding or reputation management, a strong list of recommendations from your current employers and team leaders boasting your finer points will provide evidence to your reader that you truly are a high performing, impressive professional. If you are promoting your business, products or services, having recommendations from your current clients touting your strengths will impress your prospects.

You may be thinking, "What's the point? Every recommendation on LinkedIn® is glowing! How can there be any merit to it?"

Here's the secret, it is not what the recommendation says… it's who wrote it. Ultimately, it's all about who you know. The short recommendation from someone in a high place is significantly better than the glowing recommendation from a cashier at the local Walmart.

It is easy for your reader to find out how significant or insignificant the person is who wrote your recommendation. Clicking on the recommender's name leads to their LinkedIn® profile where your reader can then read more about their role and experiences.

Clearly, not all recommendations carry the same level of importance. The best kind of recommendation comes from employers, VIPs, or customers. Recommendations by colleagues and people in lateral positions are useful but not nearly as powerful.

The Ranking of Recommendation Writers

1.   Employers, VIPs
2.   Customers
3.   Colleagues, partners, people in lateral positions
4.   Fans, vendors, friends, family members

Who to Ask for a Recommendation?

Who should you ask for a recommendation? Here are some questions to help you identify the right people:

- Who have you mentored? Who has mentored you?

- Who has helped you? Who have you helped?

- Who has a large LinkedIn® network? Who is active on LinkedIn®? Who shares your target audience?

- Who inspires you?

Are people coming to mind? Don't feel shy about asking for a recommendation. People love helping other people and you may even find people are tickled that you asked them to recommend you.

When asking for a recommendation, I highly suggest writing the recommendation yourself because you can rest assured the recommendation is written with all the points you want covered. Additionally, by writing the recommendation yourself, you can infuse the recommendation with keywords that will optimize your profile's searchability. We'll get into search engine optimization a little later on so don't worry too much about it just yet. People often balk when I suggest providing a person with a prewritten recommendation.

"How ballsy! Won't the person be insulted?"

No! The other person is going to be overjoyed. Most people don't have the time, inclination, or ability to write you a recommendation. I hate this to be a wakeup call but people have much better things to do with their lives than write you a LinkedIn® recommendation. Since this person is doing you a favor, how about doing them a favor by making it as easy for them as possible to help you.

If you are totally against writing the recommendation yourself, at the very least provide the person with some criteria as to what you'd like them to state in their recommendation:

> When you write the recommendation, I would love it if you'd mention my strength in solution selling and how I often acted as a trusted advisor to my clients. Perhaps you can even mention how I saved the Kapinsky deal using my knowledge of widgets and ended up renewing them for an extra 3 years which resulted in an additional $2M in revenue?

The Perfect Recommendation

When writing a recommendation for yourself the best thing to do is list your qualities you want highlighted. You can also ask yourself the following questions:

- How does this person know you? How long have you known each other? How did you work together?
- Detail a singular experience in which you exhibited a high level of leadership as it fits within their knowledge of you.
- What one quality of yours proved beneficial to this person? What was the result?

- Did you mentor this person? What impact did this mentoring have on them?

Use the answers to these questions to craft a powerful recommendation.

Requesting a Recommendation

You can request a recommendation in a number of ways but the easiest way is:

1. Click Profile on LinkedIn®'s top navigation bar.
2. Click the arrow icon within the gray button at the top section of your profile and select, Ask to be recommended.
3. Follow the prompts and write your own recommendation for the person.
4. Click Send.

Your request for a recommendation is sent as a LinkedIn® message and as an email.

When requesting a recommendation from a connection, LinkedIn® provides a pre-written request for you to send. Guess what? I recommend ditching LinkedIn®'s default text and writing your own. Try something like this:

Recommendation Request Template Text

It's been such a pleasure working with you over the past few months. Since you've been such a fantastic client, I would love to include a recommendation from you on my LinkedIn® profile. In order to make this process as easy as possible, I have written the recommendation for you. Please feel free to make any edits and if you would prefer to write your own recommendation, please do so. Thank you for in advance.

Although you may think it's a great idea, don't email the request for a recommendation outside of LinkedIn®. This will make it difficult for your contact to figure out how to provide the recommendation. Send the request from inside LinkedIn®. This way your contact can easily click the link that LinkedIn® provides, making it easy for them to give you a recommendation.

Once the recommendation request is sent out, you can certainly lean back and wait for a response but a more proactive approach is to reach out to the person directly and let them know that you requested a recommendation. Walk them through the steps of providing the recommendation and let them know how appreciative you are of the help they are providing.

Accepting a Recommendation

LinkedIn® sends an email notification when you receive a recommendation. This email contains a preview of the recommendation. Once you have reviewed it, there are three options listed in the email.

First, you can choose to Accept the Recommendation and have it shown on your profile.

The second option is to request a replacement of the recommendation. This is used if the recommendation has a typo or if you want to request an edit. I know it may feel weird to request a replacement but it's an important thing to do. You don't want to publish a recommendation filled with typos. That would defeat the purpose of the recommendation.

The third option is to archive the recommendation which simply means you choose to ignore it. It may seem odd to ignore a recommendation but I have archived and ignored many recommendations. If the person recommending you has a poor reputation or the recommendation isn't authentic or genuine, it is best to simply archive it.

Recommendations for Others

You recognize the importance of getting recommendations but it's also just as important to give recommendations to people. Think about it, you want to brand yourself as a leader and executive. Leaders and executives don't just get recommendations, *they give them*!

Most people wait until asked to give a recommendation... but not you! I say, incorporate giving recommendations into your process. Once a month, look back and determine who did good by you. Who inspired and impressed you? Out of the kindness of your heart, send them a glowing recommendation. You will be surprised by the karma you receive.

In fact, writing recommendations for others is a great way to promote yourself. Yes, it is true! When writing a recommendation, introduce yourself and explain what you do. Not only does this give the recommendation context and credibility, it also serves to get the word out about you.

Recommendation Example

> *As a Web Designer, I work with many non-profits; creating dynamic and affordable Websites they can maintain themselves.* I have frequently referred Stephen X to my non-profit accounts that need help with fundraising. The feedback my clients provide me regarding Stephen is very positive. Stephen is a truly inspirational person and the work he does is special, making a difference in each organization he helps. I heartily recommend Stephen X as a key figure in fundraising for non-profits

People who read this recommendation may find themselves curious about the awesome person providing the recommendation and they will click on your profile to learn more about you.

Giving a Recommendation

1.   Search LinkedIn® for the person you want to recommend.
2.   Open their LinkedIn® profile.
3.   Scroll down to the Recommendation section of their LinkedIn® profile and choose Recommend.
4.   Follow the prompts and create your recommendation.
5.   Click Send.

The Ripple Effect

When you accept a recommendation, it ripples throughout your network and the network of the person who gave it. This recommendation is being seen by all sorts of people as it is broadcast out as a network update. As your recommendation ripples out, you are gaining views from people outside your network and you are staying top of mind to those who share your network. You never know where opportunity might be found. Many of my clients came to me by reading recommendations given to me by their connections. I have also gained new clients from people who read my recommendations and were curious to learn more about me, the person giving the recommendation.

A Tip for Sales Professionals and Entrepreneurs

How many times have you heard the words, "I'd love to move forward with your product/service but first I need to talk to some of your customers. Can you provide me with a list of happy clients?"

Next thing you know, you have spent several hours calling clients to see if they are open to talking to your prospect and preparing a list of names, titles, and phone numbers. Finally you send it off to your prospect, only for them to file it away without reaching out to any of the people on the list. You have just wasted your time and your customers' time.

If you keep your LinkedIn® Recommendation section up to date with client recommendations, think how easy the reply to your prospect could be: "Sure, visit my LinkedIn® page. I have over 100 recommendations from happy customers. Feel free to reach out to them via LinkedIn® ... so shall I submit your order for the blue or green widgets?"

12

Additional Informational

Interests ★ Personal Details
Advice for Contacting

Additional Information

The Additional Information section is where you tell people more about yourself. It is where you list your interests, personal details, and advice for contacting you. This section provides your reader with a well-rounded view of you as a person, both professionally and personally. It allows your reader to develop a professional rapport with you while creating the basis for a more personal relationship.

Editing the Additional Information Section

1. Click Profile > Edit Profile on LinkedIn®'s top navigation bar.
2. Scroll down to Additional Information.
3. Click the edit icon to the right of Interests.

Interests

The Interests section is where you add your hobbies and personal interests to your LinkedIn® profile. By letting your reader see your avocations, you are allowing them to connect with you on a more personal level.

I often hear from clients, "But Donna, I don't feel comfortable listing my hobbies and interests!"

Think about it, what's the first thing you do when you walk into another person's office that you don't know very well? You look around! You look for pictures, plaques, trophies, toys and other objects that will give you fodder for conversation. You may even find yourself exclaiming, "Oh, I see you fish... I love deep water fishing. Have you been to Bermuda?" This is how you forge a connection and build a relationship.

The Interests section is where you let your reader connect with you at a deeper level. This shows your reader you have a life outside of work and are not just a corporate creature.

Here's an example:

> **Interests:** Volunteering at soup kitchens, traveling outside the US, outdoors-lover, hiking, rafting, reading books on sales, body language, and psychology.

Make this section your own and infuse it with some personality. Shine! But be careful. You don't want to come across as a flake. The interests that you choose should reflect the characteristics a person in your desired role/field should exude. Prove you are the leader you say you are by choosing interests that reflect the qualities of a leader, like Bayliner Captain, Little League Coach or Grand Poobah of the Loyal Order of Water Buffalo. If you want to appear technically savvy, mention that you enjoy gadgets, building computers, or coding Websites for non-profit organizations.

To make this easy, I've included on the next page, a list of interests categorized by the traits they exude to help you.

Interests Picker

Leader

- Coaching Little League
- Entrepreneurship
- Community Association Board President
- Sailboat Captain

Giver

- Philanthropy
- Volunteer work
- Charity work
- Helping the disadvantaged

Focused

- Investments
- Coin Collector
- Stamp Collector
- Model Airplanes

Intelligent

- History
- Personal Development
- Reading Books
- Writing
- Chess

Healthy

- Sports
- Sailing
- Gym Nut
- Hiking
- Swimming

Tech Savvy

- Blogging
- Web Design
- Gadgets
- Electronics

Adventurous

- Rafting
- Travel
- Flying
- Zip lining
- Rock Climbing
- Luger

Well-Rounded

- Museums
- Spending time with my kids
- Cooking, Baking
- Wine Tasting

Flaky

- Unleashing my inner Liza!
- Picking belly button lint

It is worth noting that you should separate your interests with commas. You see, LinkedIn® automatically links your interests to other profiles that share the same interests as you. This is a great way to find people with common interests that you can add to your network. Let's test this out.

Viewing Your Interest Hyperlinks

1. Save your changes to the Additional Profile section.
2. Click Profile on LinkedIn®'s top navigation bar and scroll down to the Additional Information section.

Notice how your interests are underlined. By separating your interests with commas, LinkedIn® knows what words should be hyperlinked. If you don't include commas, the entire phrase becomes one giant hyperlinked group of words connecting you to no one. Go ahead, click on an interest. The resulting page will be a list of other professionals who share that interest with you.

Personal Details

The next two fields within the Additional Information section are your birthday and marital status. If you decide to enter information into these fields, LinkedIn® gives you the opportunity to determine who can see it by clicking on the little icon in the shape of a lock. Your options are:

- Everyone
- Just Your Connections
- Just Your Network

By selecting Everyone, anyone who views your profile, regardless of their LinkedIn® connection to you, can see the contents of the field. Selecting Just Your Connections, only people who are directly connected to you can see it. If you choose Just Your Network, anyone who is connected to you, plus their connections, and their connections' connections can see it.

Are there repercussions to letting people know your age and marital status? Of course! If you are not comfortable letting people know these things, leave the fields blank.

If you are married, you may want to consider listing your marital status because in most people's minds being married conveys stability and maturity and that's not a bad thing to have people assume.

Age Discrimination

People often ask if I suggest omitting all dates from their LinkedIn® profile to offset potential age discrimination. If you are looking for a job and you omit dates, it's a red flag to recruiters and hiring managers who will pass by your profile quicker than the little old lady from Pasadena. They aren't discriminating against you because of your age but because you aren't providing accurate information.

Omitting dates is not a good idea. But let's say you do it and somehow manage to get asked to interview at a company that devalues age. Your crow's feet and silver hair will give away your real age when you show up at the door. It doesn't matter if you interview great, you will never get the job. Age discrimination is out there and it's ugly but there are plenty of companies who value your wisdom and experience.

I say showcase your true self on your LinkedIn® profile and get discriminated against up front so you don't waste your time with a close-minded company who doesn't respect you. The good companies that realize your value and strengths are out there and those are the companies to pursue.

Advice for Contacting

Now it's time to provide future readers of your profile with advice on how to best connect with you. Success on LinkedIn® is getting off LinkedIn®. It's the real world where strong relationships are forged. This is the section where you let your reader know why and how to contact you. I often use:

> I am always open to a conversation. Connect with me on LinkedIn® and we can set up a time to talk.

You can also opt for a little more enthusiasm, if you'd like:

> I welcome all calls and emails. You can reach me at 555-7643 or hellodolly@hotmail.com - I look forward to hearing from you.

Additional Information Example

Interests

Health nut, vegetarian, animal lover, amateur pilot, gardener, reader of books on self-help, marketing, and sales techniques.

Personal Details

Birthday   August 1

Marital Status   Married

Advice for Contacting You

I'm always open to a conversation. Please feel free to add me to your LinkedIn® network. You can reach me via email at DollyMadison@Yahoo.com or by phone at 555-555-1234.

11

Education & More

The Academics ★ Activities and Societies
Description ★ The Uneducated Masses
All-Star Profile ★ Sending Invitations

Education

The Education section is where you proudly announce your alma mater to your reader.

Editing the Education Section

1. Click Profile > Edit Profile on LinkedIn®'s top navigation bar.
2. Scroll down to the Education section.
3. Either click the + Add education link to the right of Education to add a new school or click the edit icon to revise the information already listed.

The first field to fill out is School Name. As you start typing the name of your school, a drop list will appear. By selecting your school from the drop list, you are using its standardized name so LinkedIn® can link you to other graduates from the same school.

The next fields to fill out are Dates Attended, Degree, Field of Study, and Grade.

One thing I have noticed over and over again is people tend to omit the years they attended school. I suppose the reason is twofold, either they prefer to disguise their real age or they do not want people to realize that it took them more than the usual amount of time to graduate.

I say, "Don't worry about it!" Embrace your age; embrace your ability to stick with your education regardless of how long it took to achieve that diploma.

By putting the years you attended university, you are letting LinkedIn® know who else graduated with you. This means more people to add to your network. And that's a good thing.

I remember one of my clients resisted adding the date of her college graduation. I insisted it would help her connect with fellow graduates and provide her with potential business opportunities. Finally she relented and we added her graduation date to her profile. Wouldn't you know that within a few days, she began receiving invitations to connect from fellow alumni? One of those new connections now owned a small business and was looking for someone with her experience. She received an interview and a job simply by adding her graduation date to her profile.

If you are really against showing the full term of your education, at the very least, enter the year you graduated. This way you can still connect with your fellow graduates without divulging too much information.

The Grade field is a relatively new field. For the life of me I can't figure out what made LinkedIn® think this is a field that anyone would fill out. Leave it blank unless you are one of the minority who graduated at the top of their class… in that case, brag!

The last two fields to fill out are Activities & Societies and Description. It is very tempting to leave these fields blank but try to resist. Profiles that are completely filled out rank better than profiles missing information. This means you should enter *something* in these fields.

Cast your mind back and reminisce about those heady days at university. What activities did you participate in? Were you in a fraternity or sorority? Did you belong to any clubs? Determine the activities that portray you as a well-rounded individual and list them.

Activities & Societies: Foreign Language Club, Debate Team, Football, Grecian Wrestling, Theater, Delta Delta Delta Sorority, Chess Club

The Description field is where you provide information on your educational background and experience. Did you graduate with honors? Were you the recipient of a scholarship? Take the most interesting notes and add them into your profile.

Description: Fulbright Scholarship. Graduated cum laude. Study Abroad Program, Junior Year, London, England.

Hey, you look a little glassy-eyed. Are you sure you don't have any additional notes to list? It's important to list something... *anything*.

How about:

Nontraditional-aged student, spent down time with family.

or

Matriculated while working full time.

or

Thesis entitled, Liberation of Literature during Fin de siècle France

or

Minored in English, concentrated in American Literature.

or

Earned my degree while drinking heavily and having the time of my life.

Okay, maybe not that last one.

Education is certainly important but it is not the place to spend too much time fretting over. Your experience and skillsets will open doors for you, so finish up this section and let's move on to the more exciting parts of your profile.

The Uneducated Masses

And now for those of you who opted not to attend college but decided instead to hire someone who did... this is where it gets tricky. I do not suggest skipping this section since it does have a bearing on the completeness of your profile. My recommendation is to scroll through the School Name drop list and choose Other. Enter your high school information or whatever was the last bit of education you received.

Heck, if you must, you can always enter: *The Esteemed School of Hard Knocks*. You must put something in the School Name field. You will never reach 100% profile completeness without the Education section filled in. We will talk more about the importance of a complete profile in the next section.

Education Example

School
Rosemont College

Dates Attended
1992 to 1996

Degree
BA

Field of Study
Humanities

Grade
4.0

Activities and Societies
Foreign Language Club, Jest and Gesture, Yearbook, etc...

Description
Graduated summa cum laude.

Achieving a Complete Profile

Users with complete profiles are 40 times more likely to receive opportunities through LinkedIn® than someone with an incomplete profile. This means you will connect with more people and truly experience the benefits of LinkedIn®.

I have found that complete profiles rank higher in LinkedIn®'s search results. LinkedIn® wants to ensure their search results are accurate and so it makes sense that they promote profiles that are completely filled out ahead of profiles that are incomplete.

Think of it this way, why would LinkedIn® promote profiles to the top of search results that are half-filled out? LinkedIn® isn't that much different from Google. The power is in the search results. If the results are worthless, people will go elsewhere.

In order to combat poor search results, LinkedIn® put into place a benchmark based upon the completeness of your profile. Click Profile on LinkedIn®'s top navigation bar and look to the right hand side of the page to see the graphic that shows the strength of your profile. Your profile may be one of the following:

- Just Starting
- Beginner
- Intermediate
- Expert
- All-Star, 100%

Clearly, you want to aim for an All-Star profile. The items that make a profile All-Star are:

- Your industry and location
- An up-to-date current position (with a description)

- Two past positions
- Your education
- Your skills (minimum of 3)
- A profile photo
- At least 50 connections

As you continue through this book, I will ensure you meet all of these criteria.

Getting Your First 50 Connections

The area that causes the most difficulty in getting to a 100% complete profile is connecting with 50 people.

Here are some ideas of people you can invite to connect on LinkedIn®:

- Friends
- Family
- Current Colleagues
- Past Colleagues
- Current Employer
- Past Employers
- Alumni

Once you identify the right people, it's time to ask them to connect.

Sending a LinkedIn® Invitation

1. Enter the person's name in the search box located within the top navigation bar and click enter on your keyboard.
2. Find the person in the resulting search results. You may have to filter for city or company if there are hundreds of people with the same name.

3.   Click their name to open their LinkedIn® profile.
4.   Once in their profile, click Connect.
5.   Follow the prompts.
6.   Click Send.

LinkedIn® provides you with a canned message for your invitation. Rather than keep the default text, I recommend customizing with your own words:

Personalized LinkedIn® Invitation

I don't know if you remember me but we worked together at Widgets Inc. about 5 years ago. You always impressed me with your amazing project management ability. Now that I am on LinkedIn®, I would love to connect with you and get back in touch.

When you do finally achieve a complete, All-Star profile, the sense of accomplishment is fantastic. When it happens, you must go out and celebrate, knowing that your profile is more likely to appear in LinkedIn® search results.

10

Additional Profile Sections

Honors & Awards ★ Organizations ★ Certifications ★
Languages ★ Volunteer Experiences & Causes
Publications ★ Patents ★ Projects
Courses ★ Test Scores

Additional Profile Sections

Certain professions demand certain skillsets, certifications, and abilities. The Additional Profile sections gives you the ability to further optimize your profile by adding Organizations, Honors & Awards, Volunteer Experiences & Causes, Projects, Publications, Certifications, Languages, Courses, or Test Scores.

Adding Additional Profile Sections

1.   Click Profile > Edit Profile on LinkedIn®'s top navigation bar.
2.   On the right side of the screen, click the plus sign next to the profile section you wish to add.

Each section is added separately. Once added, these sections populate your profile right above the Recommendations section. After all the sections are added to your profile, you can edit them by clicking the edit icon next to the section name. You can even rearrange sections by clicking the up-down arrow next to the section you'd like to move. Drag the section to a new location and release your mouse button to position it in the new area.

LinkedIn® often changes its interface. These directions may change. If the directions don't make sense, don't panic. Visit my Website, http://www.LinkedIn-Makeover.com for updated directions.

Organizations

Don't get the Organizations section mixed up with LinkedIn® Groups. Organizations are real world associations and clubs to which you belong. Listing organizations on your LinkedIn® profile shows you are an integral part of your community and that you are involved in your industry.

You can determine the organizations to list on your profile by asking yourself the question, "What industry organizations do I belong to?" Are you a member of Rotary, or a networking group? Maybe you are an active member of the local Chamber of Commerce? Do you sit on a board of directors? Add each organization separately.

Organization Example

Organization: Canterbury Croft Community Association

Positions Held: Secretary

Occupation: Account Manager at Design, LLC

Time Period: March 2009 – August 2012

Additional Notes: Canterbury Croft condominiums in Village Shires is located in Bucks County, PA and consists of 74 condominium units. As the secretary, I am responsible for ensuring that accurate minutes of the meetings are taken and approved.

Honors and Awards

The Honors and Awards section is the area to enter any honors and awards you earned throughout your career. Don't go too far back! If you are over 20, no one wants to read about your Little League days.

Awards to List	Awards to Avoid
Software Salesperson of the Year, 2008	Little League Good Sport Award, 1974
Golden Apple Award for Outstanding Teacher, 2007	Student of the Month 1981
Who's Who in America, 1999-2008	Dishonorable Discharge 2001
President's Club, 2000-2012	Darwin Award Recipient for tragic helium balloon & lawn chair incident

Yes, I know you have been far too busy getting the ball to the other side of the court to bother yourself with documenting the honors and awards you received. I say STOP! Stop and look around. If you don't record these honors, no one else will. You never know when it might come down to you and another highly lauded individual for a job, promotion, or project. You don't want to miss out simply because they recorded and touted their accomplishments and you didn't.

One more thing, honors and awards aren't just bestowed on just anyone. Honors and awards are typically given to people who have asked for recognition. You control how people perceive you. It's time for you to start strategically identifying honors and awards and doing what it takes to obtain them. Make sure it's known that you are interested and worthy. Keep an eye out for initiatives where you can volunteer to be seen. Honors and awards prove to your audience that you have what it takes to be a success and deserve recognition.

I remember working with a woman on her LinkedIn® profile and she said she didn't have any honors or awards that were pertinent to her career. I noticed a plaque on the wall and asked her about it. Turns out she had received this plaque by an airline for coming to the aid of passengers during a plane crash... *and she didn't think it was worthwhile to put this honor on her profile!* This is a fantastic honor and although it had nothing to do with her career, it did show her to be a heroic person who clearly works well under pressure. And so, indirectly, it had everything to do with her career.

Here are some other ideas....

Did you ever receive one of those silly awards Corporate America loves to hand out instead of bonuses? I was once the proud recipient of the Wedge Award. Who ever heard of the Wedge Award? No one other than the VP at my old company, that's who. I still listed it on my profile. Rather than just listing its name, I added a little description to it.

> The Wedge Award was awarded to individuals who helped increase the "wedge" between profit and expenses.

Think beyond the certificate, plaque, and trophy. Were you ever quoted in a newspaper article? Perhaps you delivered a keynote address to an organization? These are fantastic items to list under Honors and Awards.

> Delaware County Chamber of Commerce Annual Meeting Speaker

> Quoted in Oregon County Intelligencer article on Green Building Practices

By adding your honors, regardless of how silly they may seem to you, potential employers or customers will take notice. No one else will toot your horn so it's important you do it.

Honors & Awards Example

Title: Young Entrepreneur Profile

Occupation: Owner, Vision Board Media

Issuer: Philadelphia Business Journal

Date: July 2010

Description: The Philadelphia Business Journal is a weekly business-oriented newspaper published in Philadelphia, Pennsylvania. Once a year, the Philadelphia Business Journal profiles a young entrepreneur who has experienced success in their industry. I was chosen for the work I had done in educating small businesses on Social Media.

Certifications

Certifications play a big role in certain careers. LinkedIn® provides you the ability to list certifications, licensures, and clearances directly on your profile.

People tend to confuse the Education and Certifications sections. If you received a degree, then you want to list that as education. If you received a certificate or a certification, then you want to list it as a certification.

Education	Certification
Accounting	CPA
Information Technology	Microsoft Certified
MBA	Leadership Program

This section is where you list the certifications that are pertinent to your field. If you have a certification that no longer plays a role in your career, leave it off. If License Number does not pertain to your certification, feel free to leave it blank. If you do not have any certifications, don't fret. You do not need to add this section to your profile.

Certifications Example

Certification Name: LEED Certification

Certification Authority: Green Building Certification Institute (GBCI)

License Number: 42819

Dates: January 2011-2012

Languages

By adding the Languages section to your LinkedIn® profile, you can brag about the number of languages you speak to even more people than just the hipsters who attend your dinner parties.

Simply choose your language from the drop list and then choose your level of proficiency.

You can choose from:

- Elementary proficiency
- Limited working proficiency
- Professional working proficiency
- Full professional proficiency
- Native or bilingual proficiency

If you do add a foreign language to this section, also add your native language, as well. You don't want a potential alliance to dismiss you because they assume you hired a translator and don't speak their language.

Languages Example

Language	Proficiency
English	Native or bilingual proficiency
German	Elementary proficiency

Publications

Are you a writer? Have you been published? The Publications section of LinkedIn® is the place to add your published work.

The Publications section is a great place to get the word out on your writing and show the world you are an expert. Do not think this section is only for books you have written. If you wrote an article that was broadcast in some manner, add it to this section and share it with the readers of your LinkedIn® profile. You can cite magazine articles, newsletter pieces, guest blog articles, etc...

Publications Example

Title: Professional Tips to a POWERFUL LinkedIn® Profile

Publication/Publisher: Bycko Press

Publication Date: June 2013

Publication URL: http://www.LinkedIn-Makeover.com

Author: Donna Serdula

Summary: Learn how to create a powerful LinkedIn® profile, quickly and easily with this fun book straight from the pen of a professional LinkedIn® Profile Writer. Be noticed, get hired, and find business TODAY.

Patents

A patent is a professional accomplishment and should be shared on your profile. If you are an inventor with patents to your name, you can list them in the Patent section of your LinkedIn® profile.

If you don't have any patents, don't add this section to your profile.

Patents Example

Patent Office: Swedish Patent and Registration Office

Status of Patent: Patent Issued

Patent/Application Number: 3344295

Patent Title: Widgetizer

Issue/Filing Date: January 2011

Patent URL: http://www.widgetizer555.com

Inventor: Marvin Widgman

Summary: The Widgetizer splits widgets into tiny widgets

Projects

You can list projects on your profile. This section is perfect to spotlight your involvement in company-driven initiatives. This is also a place for consultants to list their work with companies where they worked but not as an employee.

This section also allows you to add a URL and additional team members.

Projects Example

Name Sarbanes Oxley Compliance

Occupation Financial Auditor

Date Range 2004-2006

Project URL http://WidgetsInc.com/SarbanesProject

Team Member(s)* Sheldon Nickel, Ryan Tornatelli, Jane Skylar

Description Created a team to achieve Sarbanes-Oxley compliance while utilizing this opportunity to improve overall risk management and business performance. Within a 2 year period, we achieved complete compliance while streamlining processes.

Courses

Are you one of those people who are devoted to their own personal development? You can list courses on your profile to showcase your continuing education. Rather than simply adding a degree or certification, you can list the actual courses you have taken that are pertinent to your career.

If you are currently working toward a degree, you can add a few courses that showcase your course load.

Courses Example

Course Name*	Number	Associated with
Web Marketing	101	Webmaster, WidgetsInc.com
Financial Audits	101	Financial Analyst, DK Designs
Copywriting	101	Product Manager, HAL, Inc

Test Scores

Although most profile sections are designed specifically for professionals, LinkedIn® included this section especially for students. Are your standardized test scores a thing of beauty? Don't keep them to yourself. List those scores on your LinkedIn® profile and impress your readers.

Test Scores Examples

Name TOEIC Speaking Test:

Occupation Facilities Manager, Widgets Inc

Score 905

Date January 2012

Description Scored 905 on the Test of English for International Communication (TOEIC). Achieved a top score level rating of able to communicate effectively in almost any situation.

9

SEO & More

Search Engine Optimization ★ Skills & Expertise
Endorsements

LinkedIn® Profile SEO

LinkedIn® is much more than just a social network for business people. It is a database of professionals for professionals.

People use LinkedIn® for more than just a professional, online profile. LinkedIn® is used to find potential customers, vendors, service providers, and employees.

Not everyone is searching for you based upon your name. More often, people are searching for particular strengths, skillsets, and abilities. And so if a person is searching LinkedIn® for someone with your qualifications, don't you want your profile to appear in their search results? Of course you do. That is why it is important to optimize your profile for LinkedIn®'s search engine. SEO stands for search engine optimization.

Keywords

When people use LinkedIn®'s search functionality to find a person with a particular set of qualifications, they will enter descriptive words into LinkedIn's advanced search page... words that should appear within their target's LinkedIn® profile.

In order to appear in search results, you must identify what words people are using to find a person with your qualifications and abilities. What words would they type into the LinkedIn® search engine to find you? These search terms are your keywords.

Your profile will never appear in search results for terms that do not appear in your profile. In order to appear, your profile must contain those keywords people use for search.

I was once contacted by an Accountant who wanted to know why she never received any business inquiries from her large LinkedIn® network. I looked at her profile and noticed she only referred to herself as CPA. I asked how her clients referred to her.

"My clients call me their Accountant."

"Then why isn't Accountant listed anywhere on your profile? If a person searches for Accountant on LinkedIn®, your profile will never show up because that keyword doesn't exist on your profile."

She was shocked that she could have missed something so simple. We talked further and I learned she is often approached by people for tax preparation and financial audits. Once we included these additional keywords on her profile, she suddenly started to get business inquiries from her network.

Keyword Density

As you move through the rest of your profile, it is important that you naturally use these keywords in your narrative. Write for your reader first and the search engine second.

The more times a keyword is repeated, the higher you rank for that keyword in LinkedIn® search results. Repeating keywords is clearly a good thing. However, it's easy to slip into obnoxiousness when you repeat keywords.

Non-Obnoxious Keyword Repetition	Obnoxious Keyword Repetition
As an account manager & sales person who specializes in the sales & marketing of architectural software, I utilize solution selling and consultative selling in my sales process.	Sales, sales...

Sure you can rank high by repeating your keywords ad nauseam but what happens when a prospect opens your profile and sees the repetition? They will be disgusted by your audacity and will exit from your profile and move on to the next search result. Keyword abuse doesn't impress anyone.

Rather than go crazy adding keywords willy nilly through your profile, it's best to be strategic. There are certain areas within your LinkedIn® profile that are weighted more heavily in the eyes of LinkedIn®'s search engine.

High Impact SEO Fields

- Headline
- Summary
- Skills & Expertise
- Job Titles (especially current)
- Job Descriptions

Make sure these five areas are rich in your chosen keywords.

How many keywords do you need? I say choose five to ten keywords to pepper throughout your profile, concentrating on the high impact SEO fields. The more keywords you use, the harder it will be to achieve a good density of keywords in the text. It is possible to optimize for more keywords but a good, safe goal is five.

It's important to note, keywords don't have to be just one word. It could be a phrase. Profit and loss may be three words but it is one keyword.

Here are some questions to help you find your keywords:

- What industries have you worked?

- What positions have you held?
- What certifications have you earned?
- What skill sets were listed on your last job description or resume?
- What computer applications do you know?
- What languages do you speak?

Please take note, problem solver is not a keyword. Dynamic professional is not a keyword. Results-oriented? Not a keyword either. Keywords need to be very specific to you. They should also be reflective of key skills, competencies, specialties, abilities that you possess.

I know it's tough to determine keywords so I am going to give you two tools to help ferret them out.

One of my secret weapons to find keywords is… the word cloud. A word cloud is a weighted list of words in visual form. My favorite word cloud generator is Wordle.net but there are others out there:

- http://www.tagxedo.com/
- http://worditout.com/

In order to use a word cloud generator you first need to find text to pump into it. I suggest obtaining either your own job description in digital format or finding a similar job description online. Heck, rather than getting your current job description, you could even do a search for your dream job description. Don't worry whether the position is in your area or already filled. Most job descriptions are the same—you are just after the wording not whether it's a real opportunity.

Now that you have the job description, copy the text and paste it into any word cloud generator. The resulting word cloud will visually show you what words hold the highest authority. These words are typically your keywords.

You don't need to stick to just job descriptions. You can copy and paste LinkedIn® profiles, articles, white papers or other text into the word cloud generator. The idea is to find the keywords people are using to find someone like you.

I will admit, word clouds are hit or miss. Sometimes the results are amazing, sometimes... not so much. If your word cloud provided you a good strong list of keywords, awesome! If not, no worries. I have another secret weapon for you.

You are going to visit an area of LinkedIn® I bet you never visited before.... The Skills & Expertise page.

The Skills & Expertise page is not accessible from LinkedIn®'s navigation bar and because of that most people are not aware it exists. This page allows you to discover the skills you need to succeed in this crazy world.

Accessing Skills & Expertise

1.   In the address bar of your browser, type:
     http://www.linkedin.com/skills/ and click the enter or
     return key on your keyboard
2.   The Skills & Expertise page will display.

Once at the Skills & Expertise page, the first thing you will see is a giant search box. Type in your job title or your area of expertise. As you type, you may notice that LinkedIn® tries to guess what you are going to type and they provide you with even more keyword ideas.

Click the Search button and LinkedIn® will show you a definition of that skill. Look over to the left hand side of the page. Notice how LinkedIn® provides you a list of related skills? This is where you go to town. Start clicking on the skills that look good to you. Don't add them to your profile yet... we'll get to that soon. Right now I want you to use this tool to find the keywords that best reflect you as a professional. Once you find your top 5 keywords, write them down.

So what's the point of the Skills & Expertise page? The need for certain skills is ever changing in this ever changing world. Expertise is not always easy to pinpoint and the demand for certain skills changes quickly. The Skills & Expertise area of LinkedIn® provides tracking on the trends of different skills & expertise and is based on skills that LinkedIn® users added to their profile pages.

Once you have one skill identified, you can see a list of related skills. LinkedIn® also provides you with other professionals in your network that share those skillsets. If that's not enough information, you can see the relative growth, size, and age range of users with those skills. LinkedIn® also provides a listing of companies and locations where that skill is common AND current jobs posted for that skill.

My LinkedIn® Keywords/Phrases

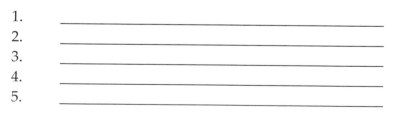

1. _____

2. _____

3. _____

4. _____

5. _____

SEO Keyword Experiment

Let's do an experiment to see just how important keyword density is in the ranking of search results.

1.   Choose your top keyword and enter it into the search box located on LinkedIn's top navigation bar and click the enter key on your keyboard.
2.   Search results for your query will appear.

Click on the #1 ranked profile. Scan the profile for your keyword. Count how many times the keyword appears in the profile. It's repeated throughout that profile, right? Over and over again. Clearly keyword density means something, huh?

If you want to outrank this person in search results, you need to pepper those keywords into your profile in even greater number.

Off Page SEO

In addition to building a powerful profile enriched with keywords, there are two other ways to increase your LinkedIn® (and Google) search ranking. Participating in LinkedIn® Group discussions increases the links back to your profile and strengthens your visibility in the eyes of the search engine. The second way to enhance your LinkedIn® search ranking is through increasing the number of connections within your LinkedIn® network.

When you did the SEO experiment and searched for your potential keywords, did you notice the highest ranking profiles were 1st, 2nd, or 3rd degree connections within your LinkedIn® network? LinkedIn® ranks the profiles of people directly related to you first. This means the more people you are connected to directly, the higher you will rank in LinkedIn® search.

Using LinkedIn® Groups to Enhance SEO

LinkedIn® Groups provide organizations and groups a forum to keep in touch with members and facilitate discussions. By using LinkedIn® Groups, you can post messages and comment on other members' messages. Each time you post a group message, you are creating a link back to your profile. When you join a group, those group members are added to your professional network. This means increased views to your profile and the ability for more people to contact you directly.

Posting a Discussion in a Group

1. Click Interests > Groups on LinkedIn®'s top navigation bar.
2. Click the group's name to open that group.
3. Within the Start a discussion or share something with the group box, enter your topic or question. Make sure you make this interesting to draw more people to read it.
4. Enter more information in the Add more details box.
5. Click Share.

What do you share in a group? You can share links to interesting articles and information on upcoming events. You can even ask for advice. However, whatever you do, don't join a group just to market yourself.

"But what am I doing on LinkedIn® if I'm not promoting myself?"

You are on LinkedIn® to add value. You are on to educate, learn, inspire and help people. Once you go in with that type of mindset, that's when good things start to happen. Over marketing yourself on a LinkedIn® Group turns people off and may even get you kicked out of the group by the group owner and moderator. Rather than constantly advertising your products and services, concentrate on adding value and helping others.

Who Has the Time?

It's time to get real. Groups are awesome and there are thousands of people out there who have grown their business and found amazing opportunity through LinkedIn® Groups. With that said, there is only so much time in the day. I don't want you to feel that you have to be active in every single group you joined. Strategically, you joined 50 groups mainly so you could add those group members to your LinkedIn® network. Choose one or two LinkedIn® Groups that contain your target audience for your focus. Get into the habit of checking out the group discussions once a week. Participate as you can. Add discussions and comment on already occurring discussions as you see fit. And guess what? If you simply don't have enough time to keep up with one group, don't worry about it. You can still find amazing benefit from LinkedIn® without participating in groups.

Skills & Endorsements

Skills & Expertise ★ Endorsements

Skills & Expertise

Skills & Expertise is one of the newer sections of your LinkedIn® profile and it is slowly replacing the Specialties section that was located right below your LinkedIn® summary. In fact, new LinkedIn® users don't even have a Specialties section anymore. The Skills & Expertise section of your LinkedIn® profile allows you to add keywords to your profile so you can get found. LinkedIn® even states that by adding skills and expertise to your profile, you will appear in keyword searches.

Most people fill out the Skills & Expertise section by going to the Skills & Expertise section of their profile and clicking Add Skill. But not you! Instead you are going to revisit the Skills & Expertise page that you used to determine your keywords.

Adding Skills & Expertise

1. In the address bar of your browser, type: http://www.linkedin.com/skills/ and click the enter or return key on your keyboard
2. The Skills & Expertise page will display.

Remember those keywords you wrote down? We're going to use them right now. Type in your #1 keyword in the giant search box located on the Skills & Expertise page and click the Search button. LinkedIn® will then show you a definition of that skill. If that skill reflects you as a professional, you can add it to your profile by clicking the Add Skill button. Once it's listed on your profile, look over to the left hand side of the page. Notice how LinkedIn® provides you a list of related skills? Start clicking on the skills that look good to you. Add them to your profile by clicking the Add Skill button. You can add up to 50 skills on your profile. I highly recommend choosing the most descriptive skills. If that's 50 skills, that's great. If it's 20 skills, that's fine too. Once you have your skills listed, you can click the See Suggested

Skills button and LinkedIn® will provide you with a list of even more skills that people in similar positions listed on their profile.

When you hit 50 skills, LinkedIn® will no longer allow you to add more skills to your profile. If you want to add more, you must delete the older skills. Once you have all your skills added, make sure they are in the right order.

Rearranging Skills & Expertise

1.   Click Profile > Edit Profile on LinkedIn®'s top navigation bar.
2.   Scroll down to Skills & Expertise.
3.   Click the edit icon.
4.   Drag and drop the skills where you want them to appear in the list. Click the skill, making sure you keep your mouse button depressed, drag your mouse to the top or bottom of the list and then release.

Voila! You just rearranged your skills.

Endorsements

I like to call Endorsements, Recommendations Lite. Endorsements allow your direct connections to endorse you for a skill rather than typing a paragraph recommendation. Endorsements can only be given by 1st degree connections.

When giving an endorsement, you don't have to stick to the skills & expertise that person chose for themselves. You can add skills free form. This means if the person you are endorsing didn't think to peg themselves with a certain skill, you can do it for them. When you endorse a person for a skill not listed, they must approve that skill for it to appear on their LinkedIn® profile.

By endorsing people, you are showing your respect for that area of expertise they have cultivated. Think of endorsements as a thumbs up from a business acquaintance. It's a way to say, "Hey notice me because I remember and respect you."

Endorsements are a great way to showcase your own skills and a fantastic way to remind people that you recognize their strengths. The more endorsements you have on your profile, the more clout you have within the LinkedIn® world.

How to Endorse a Connection

1.   Within LinkedIn®, visit the person's profile you wish to endorse.
2.   Scroll down to the Skills & Expertise section.
3.   Hover over the skill you want to endorse and click the plus sign.
4.   You can endorse numerous skills, just keep clicking the plus signs.

Don't get carried away! Only endorse people you can authentically and honestly endorse. You will receive endorsements from people you don't know well or at all. These strangers may be endorsing you because they know of your work and wish to promote positivity in the world or they are hoping that you operate with a Quid Quo Pro mentality and you will endorse them right back. Do not feel strong-armed! Endorse people because you appreciate their work, not because you feel guilt.

How to Hide an Endorsement

Did someone unreputable endorse you for a skill? You can hide that endorsement so it doesn't show on your profile.

1.   Click Profile > Edit Profile on LinkedIn®'s top navigation bar.

2.   Scroll down to Skills & Expertise and click the edit icon.
3.   Click the Manage Endorsements link next to Add & Remove.
4.   Click a skill to show the connections who endorsed you for that skill.
5.   Uncheck the box next to any people whose endorsements you want to hide.
6.   Click Save.

Removing an Endorsement

Did you endorse someone only to learn that you would prefer to disassociate from them? You can remove that endorsement from their profile.

1.   Open your connection's profile and scroll down to Skills and Expertise.
2.   Move your cursor over the + sign next to the skill name and click it to remove your endorsement.

Don't worry; the recipient will not be notified of the removal.

Getting Endorsements

Are you not receiving endorsements from your connections? Kevin Costner was wrong when he said, "If you build it they will come." Just because you posted skills on your profile doesn't mean people will endorse you for them. If you want to showcase your strengths, you may have to prod people. You can send a simple LinkedIn® message to a few of your close connections and ask them to endorse you. Think of that old adage, "The squeaky wheel gets the oil."

Here's a template you can use:

> If you were happy with the work I performed at Widgets, Inc, would you be so kind as to endorse me on LinkedIn®?

It's just a simple click of a button. The skills and expertise I would like to be endorsed for are Project Management, Leadership Team Building, and SEO.

All you need to do is visit my profile and scroll down to the Skills & Expertise section located under my Summary.

Here's the link to my profile:
http://www.LinkedIn.com/in/todonna

Here's another option:

I just endorsed you for Project Management and Leadership Strategy on your LinkedIn® profile.

If you're comfortable with it, would you do the same for me?

There's 50 skills to choose from, all you need to do is visit my profile: http://www.LinkedIn.com/in/todonna

Endorse your 1st degree connections honestly and genuinely. No one wants to be endorsed by a stranger who is only guessing at your skills. When you make a thoughtful endorsement of a connection you know and admire, that person is more likely to return the favor in kind.

When your connections do endorse you, make sure you reach out and thank them. You can call them on the phone or send them a message via LinkedIn®.

7

Experience

Your Career Trajectory
Job Titles ★ Company Description
Accomplishments

Experience

We're getting to the fun part now.

The Experience section is the place to list your past work-related experiences to showcase the gamut of your background and your career trajectory. This is the section where you provide information on your qualifications and abilities. Most people jump right in and start adding their experiences... but not you! You're going to be strategic.

It's important that you have the right experiences listed without excessive duplication or gaps in employment history.

On the next page, I've provided a worksheet to help you determine your experiences. On this worksheet, write down the names of the companies, your titles, and the time periods you worked.

If you have a resume, you can certainly refer to it. Go ahead and start listing all your jobs. Once finished, I will show you how to figure out what jobs you need to keep and what jobs you may need to edit.

Experience List

Company Name: _____

Title: _____

Time Period: _____ ☐ keep ☐ delete ☐ edit

Company Name: _____

Title: _____

Time Period: _____ ☐ keep ☐ delete ☐ edit

Company Name: _____

Title: _____

Time Period: _____ ☐ keep ☐ delete ☐ edit

Company Name: _____

Title: _____

Time Period: _____ ☐ keep ☐ delete ☐ edit

Company Name: _____

Title: _____

Time Period: _____ ☐ keep ☐ delete ☐ edit

Company Name: _____

Title: _____

Time Period: _____ ☐ keep ☐ delete ☐ edit

Company Name: _____

Title: _____

Time Period: _____ ☐ keep ☐ delete ☐ edit

Company Name: _____

Title: _____

Time Period: _____ ☐ keep ☐ delete ☐ edit

Company Name: _____

Title: _____

Time Period: _____ ☐ keep ☐ delete ☐ edit

Company Name: _____

Title: _____

Time Period: _____ ☐ keep ☐ delete ☐ edit

Once your worksheet is filled out, look at the list through the eyes of your potential, desired readers. Are they thinking that you have too many jobs listed? Or perhaps not enough?

There is no need to list a company multiple times just to show the different positions you held. This will make it look like you jumped around a lot, especially if the reader does not notice that it is all the same company.

On the other hand, listing a company multiple times provides you with more opportunity for search engine optimization. The more job titles you have, the more keywords you can use, the higher your profile will turn up in search results for that keyword combination. You have to decide what makes most sense for you. Do you want to have a high ranking profile or do you want to showcase the time you spent with a company?

I was revamping an older gentleman's profile and he had about 10 different jobs listed for the same company. The reason he explained, was that he had worked at this company for 20 years and he was promoted a lot. We went through his positions and those that were similar we merged together. On other positions that were not too different we listed both position titles in the one field. We eventually whittled it down to 4 different positions. This way he still showed his promotions but he did not look like a dinosaur.

Alternately, I was working with a young woman on her profile. This poor gal only worked for one company. In order to reach 100% completeness, a profile needs to have 1 current and 2 past positions listed.

I was not comfortable listing her brief stint working behind the counter at Baskin & Robbins so instead, we talked and I found out she actually had been in 3 different roles within this one company. We separated out the 3 different positions so she was able to achieve a 100% complete profile and she did not look like a complete neophyte.

If you are a young whippersnapper just starting out in your career, you can list internships and volunteer positions to flesh out your experience history. As your career develops, you can delete these positions when you add newer and better positions.

Employment Gaps

Did you take time off to raise kids? Maybe you took a sabbatical? Did you nurse an ailing relative back to health? Whatever the situation, employment gaps happen. Rather than just ignoring this elephant in the room, it's best to mention it up front and provide context to your reader. You also want to show that during this down time, you stayed active in your career and community. You can list courses that you took or organizations that you participated in. This information can either go in the previous position listed or you can create a new position for the gap.

Employment Gap Example

Company Name: Health Sabbatical

Title: Marketing Manager

Time Period: January 2009 to June 2009

Description: It was in January of 2009 that I was diagnosed with cancer. The next six months were spent going through treatment and getting myself back to health. During this time, I stayed active in my career by continuing to update my blog all about social media marketing tactics. I also mentored two high school students who later enrolled in college with a degree in Marketing.

As you can see, there are no hard and fast rules when it comes to listing your past positions. You just need to be smart about it. Go through your list and determine what you want to keep and what you want to either merge or delete. Once you have your master list, move to the next section.

Experience: Putting it all together

Don't put away that company list. You're going to use it to enter your experiences directly into LinkedIn®.

Adding or Editing Experiences

1.   Click Profile > Edit Profile on LinkedIn®'s top navigation bar.
2.   Scroll down to the Experience section.
3.   Click the Add a Position link or click the edit icon to revise an existing experience.

To remove an experience that you no longer want listed on your profile, follow the steps above but click the Remove this position link at the bottom of the page.

Let's start with the newest most current experience first and then move backward in time. Your current positions are listed first and are considered the most important to your reader. It is your current role that truly defines you and not the role you performed 10 years ago. As you move back in time, you can cut some corners on content but I would never leave fields intentionally blank.

The first field on the Experience page is Company Name. As you start typing the name of your company, a drop list will appear. By selecting your company from the drop list, you are using the company's standardized name so LinkedIn® can link you to the official LinkedIn® Company page and other employees. This is also how you add the company logo next to your position. If your company is not listed in the drop list, keep typing until you finish the company name.

Creating a POWERFUL Job Title

Most people add their exact job title but this is a mistake. The job title is one of those high impact SEO fields within LinkedIn®. Rather than stating your exact job title, such as VP or Account Manager, flesh this field out with your keywords.

BEFORE Account Manager
AFTER: Account Manager ▶ Sales Professional ♦ Sales & Marketing ♦ 3D Software ♦ Digital Prototyping

BEFORE: VP
AFTER: VP / Vice-President of Sales & Marketing ▶ Strategic Relationships ♦ Business Development

If your title can be abbreviated, enter it both ways. You don't want to list yourself as VP and miss out on appearing in search results because a recruiter searched on Vice President.

There are some jobs that have titles that are rather nebulous or use terms that are just outside of the typical job title. It is acceptable to add a job title with more description to make it easier for your reader to understand. This also helps you get found by recruiters looking for specific job titles. I must caution you against exaggerating or outright lying despite the temptation.

BEFORE: Customer Development Team Member
AFTER: Customer Service Representative ▶ Client Assistance Specialist ♦ Customer Development

BEFORE: Lead Generation Specialist
AFTER: Lead Generation ▶ Cold Caller ♦ Telemarketer

There are 100 characters available in the Job Title field. Use as many of these characters as possible.

Creating Bullets

Notice how in the above examples, I've spiced up the title with symbols? This is a great way to catch the eye and provide flair.

Your LinkedIn® profile is pure text without formatting. You can't bold, italicize or underline text. All is not lost! There are more characters available to you than what you see on your keyboard. In addition to numbers, letters, and punctuation marks, there are symbols available that you can use like bullets.

Directions to get to these symbols vary depending on your operating system. The easiest way to access symbols is to visit my Linkedin® profile.

Open my profile in a new tab by clicking Ctrl-T within your browser and typing the following URL into the address bar:

http://www.LinkedIn.com/in/todonna

Once at my profile, scroll through until you get to the Projects section. I curated a list of different symbols you can use on your LinkedIn® profile simply by copying and pasting. When you find a symbol you like, highlight it, copy it, and then paste it into your profile. That's it! Easy peasy lemon squeezy.

You can use bullets for emphasis too. For instance, add bullets around your call to action or use them to break up paragraphs. Just don't go too crazy. You don't want to have too many symbols or too many different types of symbols on your profile. Remember, less is more.

Time Period

Have you jumped around from job to job a bit more than you would care to admit? You can detract from this by using just the years rather than the specific month and year in the Time Period field. Leave the month blank and input only the years. If you are still currently employed, check the box for I Currently Work Here.

Company Description

Once you get to Description, stop! Open up a new Web browser window and type the name of your company into Google followed by the word *is*.

"MKR Design is" or "Northcross, LLC is"

Everyone knows Microsoft but not everyone knows Smith Partners. You want to make sure your reader understands your background. The easiest way to do this is to find a very brief summary of the company on Google and then copy & paste it into the Description field.

On the results page, Google should list a short description of the company:

DesignBIM Enterprises is a 3D Building Software reseller offering solutions for design engineering needs, including software, support, and training…

This brief description is very nearly perfect and you haven't even opened up their Website. Sometimes Google will fail to bring up an adequate description and in that case you will have to dig a little further and visit the company's Website to find a company summary.

Once you have the company boilerplate, all you need to do is copy and paste it into LinkedIn®'s company description and do a little tweaking.

Company Boilerplate Description Example

Company Name: DesignBIM Enterprises

Title: Account Manager ♦ Sales ♦ Marketing ♦ 3D Software

Time Period: March 2008 to August 2009

Description: DesignBIM is a 3D Building Software reseller that offers complete solutions for design engineering needs. DesignBIM specializes in software, support, and engineering services and comprehensive training programs

By providing context around your company, your reader now understands a little more about you because they know more about your company.

Are you thinking, "But I don't work for a little crappy company. I work for [insert IBM or Coca Cola or a company that everyone knows about]. Do I need to provide a summary?

Yes! I would still include a brief summary. It will show humility and endear you to your reader. Plus, if a company is really huge, take the opportunity to describe the division where you worked.

Finishing up the Description

It's now time to summarize your role and accomplishments within the company.

Remember what I said about referring to your resume? Put it aside. I do not want you regurgitating your resume here.

Whatever you do... do not copy & paste your resume!

Your LinkedIn® profile is not your resume. Your resume is your career history. It's dull, boring and often task-based. Your LinkedIn® profile is your career future. Your LinkedIn® profile should be engaging and impressive to your reader. It should compel them to pick up the phone and call you. It's who you are, how you help people, and why you deserve to be noticed. A powerful LinkedIn® profile sells you.

Rather than paste your resume, speak directly to your reader instead and tell them of your accomplishments... in an honest and genuine voice. Your narrative should sound conversational, peppy, and interesting. This means no resume speak. No silly corporate jargon. It bores people and turns them off.

You already have a description of your company; now let's create a sentence that summarizes your role within the organization. (Worksheet provided at the end of the chapter to assist you)

> As the Philadelphia Account Manager for DesignBIM, I specialized in the sale and service of 3D Building Software.
>
> I partnered with architects and engineers to assist them in obtaining the right building design software solution for their unique needs.

Here's another idea:

> I worked as both Project Director and as Regional Operations Director for Northcross Group.
>
> As Project Director, my role within the organization was to carry out projects and make sure they came in under budget, on time and within the stated objectives.

Your reader should now understand your role, now explain your responsibilities.

My responsibilities included implementing a man-machine interface program and developing risk-based assessment plans that reduced scientists' time demand by 40%.

or

I was tasked with increasing new business development, streamlining operations, and building stronger relationships with clients. I hired outside contractors, negotiated contracts, managed P & L, and oversaw the strategic planning and legal issues.

Now let's highlight your greatest accomplishment within this organization:

I was hired by RTZ to manage the production facility they recently purchased.

In a record six week period, I launched this production facility from the ground up. I was responsible for hiring and training over 200 employees, ordering materials, and developing department policies and procedures. Within 6 weeks, we were producing the same amount of widgets as their other long running plants.

If you are writing a description for a past experience, mention how the position prepared you for your current path.

The times I found most fulfilling were the hours spent mentoring and coaching individuals that I had recruited for different projects. If not for these sessions, we would not have been able to complete the projects within the time limitations or funding conditions we were up against.

It was during my tenure with Northcross Group that I realized my future was in consulting and coaching small business owners to help them succeed and find peace of mind in the sea of chaos that is often business life.

You are probably now thinking, "But what about all the things I have in my resume? There's so much I want my reader to know about me."

Please resist the urge to go overboard. You must rein yourself in. You have 2,000 characters in which to describe your position and responsibilities. Aim for around 150-300 words. You are not writing a novel. Contrary to popular belief, your LinkedIn® profile does not qualify you for a position but it may *disqualify* you. Saying more may lower your chances of getting called in for an interview. So say less!

On the other hand, do not make your description too short. You want to show that you accomplished something while you were there. So think of it as whetting your readers' appetites. A person who is interested in learning more can always request your resume.

With those words ringing in your ears, I want you to insert this sentence at the very end of the Description:

> For a detailed list of accomplishments, please request my resume.

By adding this sentence, you are so cleverly hinting in the most subversive way, that you have accomplished so much that it cannot possibly fit in the space provided. Your reader will immediately assume you have so much more to offer.

Here's a caveat: If you are a person who has a tremendous need to rank highly in LinkedIn® search, it would behoove you to use all of the 2,000 characters while making sure to generously pepper your keywords throughout your text.

On the following page, I have provided a worksheet to help you complete your experiences.

But I Don't Have a Current Position!

There is an unfortunate issue with LinkedIn®. Profiles that are All-Star, which is 100% complete, tend to perform better in search results. In order to have an All-Star profile, you must have a current position and 2 previous positions. If you are unemployed, your profile does not have a current position and so it is stuck at 95% (Expert).

There are two things you can do. You can either accept this as a temporary situation and you deal with it OR you add a current position that looks like this:

Company Name: Seeking New Opportunity

Title: Financial Analyst ▶ Forecasting ♦ Auditing ♦ Analysis

Time Period: August 2012 – current

Description: I am currently looking for my next opportunity to affect positive change within an organization that values a strong entrepreneurial spirit, creative problem solving, and a desire to succeed.

The only issue with adding a current position is that it somewhat cloaks that you are not currently employed. Recruiters are divided on this issue. Some like it, others find it devious. Ultimately, there is no right or wrong; you must decide what makes the most sense for you.

Company Description Worksheet

Provide a short description of your company:

_____

_____

_____

_____

Summarize your role with the company:

_____

_____

_____

_____

What were your primary responsibilities?

_____

_____

_____

_____

Highlight an accomplishment: (We had this issue... I suggested the following... and the results were...)

_____

_____

_____

_____

How did this position prepare you for future positions?

_____

_____

_____

_____

Don't stop! Keep going. Enter a description for ALL your positions. I know this is tedious. You can do it.

Experience #2

Provide a short description of your company:

_____

_____

_____

_____

Summarize your role with the company:

_____

_____

_____

_____

What were your primary responsibilities?

_____

_____

_____

_____

Highlight an accomplishment: (We had this issue... I suggested the following... and the results were...)

_____

_____

_____

_____

How did this position prepare you for future positions?

_____

_____

_____

_____

Experience #3

Provide a short description of your company:

_____
_____
_____
_____

Summarize your role with the company:

_____
_____
_____
_____

What were your primary responsibilities?

_____
_____
_____
_____

Highlight an accomplishment: (We had this issue... I suggested the following... and the results were...)

_____
_____
_____
_____

How did this position prepare you for future positions?

_____
_____
_____
_____

Experience Example #1

Company Name: DecisionTech

Title: Business Development Manager | Sales Representative | Account Manager

Time Period: March 2004 - June 2007

Description: DecisionTech is an IT consulting firm that specializes in business strategy, advisory services, program management, and systems integration.

My role with DecisionTech was as a Business Development and Sales Analyst. I managed business development efforts for Federal and commercial salesforces while supporting a team of 10 Account Managers and 4 inside Sales Reps.

Most people hate cold calling but I find it exciting. It was through intensive prospecting that I was able to generate over 10 qualified meetings per month with executive level decision makers. The industries I targeted included: financial services, government, service providers, and cable /wireless.

My sales pipeline averaged 10M. The typical deal size was 75K+.

For a detailed list of accomplishments, please request my resume.

Experience Example #2

Company Name: JTV Service Association

Title: Freelance Computer Programmer | Process Improvement | Coder | Business Consultant

Time Period: January 2007 – June 2007

Description: JTV Service Association is a small business specializing in widget production throughout the East Coast.

I was brought on board in 2007 as an independent contractor to assist JTV in coding a proprietary database.

JTV Service Association was struggling to keep a handle on employee training. They were looking for a customized application that would take this extremely manual task and automate it.

I coded an Access database that recorded the different types of training, tracked which employees were trained and then reported the results.

This database made the job of the HR department easier since they could now easily monitor trainings and ensure they were accomplished in a timely manner.

Experience Example #3

Company Name: Rhapsodic Corporation

Title: Web Manager | Webmaster | Internet Manager | Website Information

Time Period: September 1999 to December 2009

Description: The Rhapsodic Corporation provides a wide range of products, from audiovisual and information/communication equipment to home appliances and components.

I worked at Rhapsodic for a total of 10 years. During this time I held a variety of progressively challenging positions.

My last role was Webmaster. My responsibilities included developing and managing a wide range of internet marketing tools, including promotional materials, direct-mail pieces, and Web site content.

I am most proud that during my tenure, I increased Web traffic by 28% using banner advertising and AdWords campaigns.

For a detailed list of accomplishments, please request my resume.

6

Summary

Crafting an Engaging Summary ★ Grab Your Reader's Attention
Highlight an Achievement ★ Clear Call to Action

Summary

The Summary section is where you talk about who you are and what value you add to this crazy world. This section needs to pop! POP! Do you hear me!?! This is your chance to shine. You have your reader's attention and as much as I hate to admit it, it's not very likely that your reader will read much further past your summary... that is unless you provide them with an engaging narrative that will make them want to keep reading.

Editing Your Summary

1.   Click Profile > Edit Profile on LinkedIn®'s top navigation bar.
2.   Scroll down to Summary.
3.   Click the edit icon.

Before you get ahead of yourself, you need to determine the goal of your LinkedIn® profile. Do you intend to use it to provide a professional profile on yourself? Maybe you are looking for a job? Perhaps you are a consultant and you are using your profile to sell your advisory services? Your goal will determine how you proceed from here. Just remember, your summary is an advertisement selling you.

Employment Seeker

An employment seeker is using their LinkedIn® profile specifically in their pursuit of a new job. Although many people prefer to hide their status as an employment seeker; I believe, if a person is seeking employment, they should say so. Who is going to ask you to the prom if they think you are going steady with someone else? Besides, recruiters don't take too kindly to lying.

Business Seeker

A business seeker is selling their wares on LinkedIn® and using their profile as a way to promote not just themselves but their products and services, too. Their readers are typically either customers or potential customers. What the reader learns from the profile will determine if they want to engage in future business. Ultimately the LinkedIn® profile becomes a personal sales brochure.

Reputation Seeker / Personal Branding

A reputation seeker is using their profile for reputation management and personal branding. They are not selling a product or a service or trying to find a job. Instead they are using their profile to represent themselves in the online world. Their readers may be customers, business partners, vendors, employers, recruiters, or prospective clients. The ultimate goal of a reputation seeker is to represent themselves in a manner that impresses and builds confidence in their abilities.

Your Target Audience

Now that you have decided on the goal of your LinkedIn® profile, who is your target audience? Who do you want your LinkedIn® profile to cater to? Recruiters? C-level executives? Manufacturing reps? Human Resource professionals at Pharmaceutical companies?

Imagine your target audience. What interests them? What do they want to know about you? What do you have to offer them?

The more you write for your target audience, the more successful your LinkedIn® profile will be.

I was working with a small business consultant on his LinkedIn® profile. As we brainstormed over his summary, he said to me, "I love learning from my clients. I am always learning new things from them." This sounded wonderful to him but it's not something his clients want to hear. Imagine working with a business consultant who is supposed to teach you how to run your business more successfully and you are teaching him? Beware! What sounds great to you may not sound great to your target audience.

Your reader is always thinking, "What's in it for me?" In order to have a successful LinkedIn® profile, you must be ready to tell them exactly what's in it for them. Don't be afraid to speak directly to the reader. You can use the word, you.

As an example, here's a small excerpt of my LinkedIn® profile's summary:

> You know this… People are Googling you. Your LinkedIn® profile is more often than not your digital introduction and first impression with the world. If your LinkedIn® profile doesn't showcase your skills and portray you as a polished professional, you are letting the ultimate opportunity just slip away.
>
> Do you know what makes a LinkedIn® profile stand out from the crowd?
>
> Well, I do.
>
> As a LinkedIn® Profile Writer & LinkedIn® Profile Optimization Specialist, I craft engaging, targeted, & highly compelling LinkedIn® profiles that get you NOTICED & FOUND.
>
> Stop trying to figure it out on your own and hire a LinkedIn® Profile Writer to turn your LinkedIn® profile into an amazing professional portfolio that sells YOU.

Notice how few times I say **I** and how many times I say **YOU**.

Crafting an Engaging Summary

As you go through the next few pages, keep the goal of your profile and your reader in mind. You are not chiseling your summary out of stone. At any time, you can go back and make changes. As things happen in your career, update your summary to reflect these achievements. Don't be afraid to experiment. Pay attention to the responses your profile elicits and update your profile accordingly.

How Often Should I Update my Profile?

As long as your activity feed is turned on, each time you update any part of your profile, LinkedIn® sends out an alert to your network. These updates keep you on the top of your connections' minds. Get into the habit of updating your profile at least once a month. Not only are you keeping it fresh but you are keeping yourself in front of people.

Grab Your Reader's Attention

How do you eat an elephant? One bite at a time. So let's take the first bite, okay? You are going to start your Summary section by grabbing your reader's attention.

If you are an employment or business seeker, I suggest beginning your summary with some qualifying questions. Why? Because it qualifies your reader as a potential prospect and gets them engaged fast.

What kinds of questions should you ask? Ideally questions where the answer is a resounding YES! The questions should be positive and keep the reader interested in learning more.

How do you help people or businesses? What do people love about the service you provide? Focus on efficiency, making money, achieving more, reducing costs, etc…

Here are a few examples:

Is your production packaging company looking to maximize productivity and minimize cost per case?

Are you trying to improve efficiency and reduce costs?

or

Tired of duplicate data entry?

Wish you could generate reports with a simple click of a button?

Do you want to streamline your business processes and end the manual corrections and reformatting?

or

Do you wonder how to make your business financially healthy again?

Do you dream of happy and worry- free customers?

Do you yearn to recapture the joy and pleasure your business once brought you?

or

Is your company in search of a Website manager professional who knows SEO, Web Analytics, and who can deliver projects on time and under budget with a smile on her face?

You don't have to start out with qualifying questions. Instead, come up with an attention getting opening sentence.

An attention getting opening works for employment, business and reputation seekers.

I was born with a calculator in my hand and a glint in my eye!

or

I can spot a needle in a haystack through the skills I have developed doing forensic accounting.

or

I don't fit into a standard slot. You see, I excel at building companies AND products.

or

I LOVE CUSTOMER SERVICE! Turning unhappy clients into loyal customer advocates is my specialty!

or

I've spent 25 years in the automotive industry. I started as a tire changer and I ended up in the boardroom.

Congratulations, you just got your reader's attention.

If you are unable to come up with any qualifying questions or even an attention getting opening sentence, it is okay. This next part also works as a great opener.

My Name is...

It's time to introduce yourself to your reader. Start by stating your name and summarize, in a sentence or two, what you do and why your reader should care. This may sound familiar to you… it's an elevator pitch.

An elevator pitch is a short and concise summary of what you do. The concept behind it is you are in an elevator with a VIP and you have just the amount of time it takes to ride an elevator a few floors to succinctly and compellingly explain a product, service, person, group/organization/company, or project.

When coaching people on creating a compelling elevator pitch, I ask them to imagine they are explaining what they do for a living to a small child. Simplify what you do down to the core concepts. Do not use words like contextualize, organic, synergize, or paradigm. Stay away from silly corporate jargon. Concentrate on the results you offer. It's not about what you do but how it helps people.

> My name is Don Draper and I specialize in building custom software tools that improve and streamline business processes for companies that are tired of wasting their time with redundant and manual tasks.

> or

> My name is Luke Hanz and I have over 30 years of experience in the widget packaging industry. As a professional production consultant, my role is to help businesses maximize efficiencies and productivity while reducing costs in widget production.

> or

> My name is Rosa Smith-Jones and I have spent the last 10 years measuring, managing, and reporting on Web Analytics for the likes of Widgetsoft and Widgets R Us. The good news is I am currently seeking my next opportunity.

> or

> My name is James Reddy and as a professional business coach and consultant, I help businesses in crisis. My specialty is helping to identify and solve your critical business issues then helping you implement profitable and useful solutions.

Why do you introduce yourself? It gives your reader a sense that they are really talking to you. They immediately see the profile as coming straight from your pen and not from a resume.

Avoiding Resume Speak

Don't use resume speak or corporate mumbo-jumbo. Write conversationally. Use full sentences that contain nouns and verbs.

> **Ex**. Creating a clear strategy for leveraging resources to produce the maximum number of insights possible.
> Integrating contextual analytics to business processes.
> Centralizing deep analysis expertise for use across the organizational axis but mandating each individual department and line of business takes responsibility for their own reporting needs.

I have no clue what this paragraph is about and it could be because I never got beyond the first sentence. Please do not fall into this trap. No one is impressed by such silliness.

Explain Your Benefits

Now that the reader has a general idea about who you are and what you do, it is time to talk about your benefits. How can you help your reader?

> Three years ago, I surveyed the business landscape and I noted that so many firms (from start up to Fortune 1000) struggled to build and maintain strong, high-functioning sales forces.
>
> That's why I started my company, Sales Funnel Supermen. We specialize in improving the sales process of start-up businesses as well as global enterprises.
>
> Sales Funnel Supermen provides the strategic direction and the software resources businesses need to stay competitive and profitable.
>
> or
>
> Large, complex projects that ripple throughout the organization are my specialty. I have an innate knack of being able to simplify complex ideas and break them into

smaller parts that can then be accomplished efficiently and easily. Whether it's marketing a product, building a team or entering a new market, I GET IT DONE!

or

I understand technology and can talk with the best of the developers. With that said, I am also able to communicate across all aspects of the organization. Whether its executives, call center workers, the development team or sales professionals, I get buy in and I move the initiative forward.

Here are some sentence starters:

- One of my strengths is…
- I gain immense satisfaction from…
- I am equally comfortable setting up a… or…
- My mission is to…
- My passion is…

It is important that you think in terms of your reader. What do they want to learn about you? What are they seeking? The answers to these questions will determine what you write.

If you are an employment seeker, looking for a specific job, find a job description for your desired position. Incorporate those skills and qualities the job demands into your summary. You can find job descriptions on the hiring page of a company's Website or on a job listing Website.

There is a difference between desperation and motivation. Sounding desperate in your summary is a sure way of scaring off potential employers. How do you change desperation into motivation? Go positive! Rather than talk about the job you need, tell your reader what you offer in strengths and quantifiable results.

Are you a business seeker? While your reader is scanning your profile, they are thinking, "What's in it for me?" Tell your reader how they will benefit from working with you. Include a story about a current client and what they achieved while working with you. Make the value you bring to the table clear to your reader. You want your reader to feel confident that your solution is exactly what they need.

Are you a reputation seeker? Keep your reader in mind as well. Don't be afraid to talk about your activities outside of your career. Mention your involvement in your community and your commitment to continuing your education. You are creating your own digital persona. Include the best parts of who you are and showcase them on your profile.

Highlight an Achievement

Let's now talk about a current career highlight. You don't want to get too granular as you shine the spotlight on your achievement. Keep it at the 10,000 foot level.

By highlighting an achievement, you are providing quantifiable evidence of your abilities. You want your reader to come away with a feeling of confidence that you are who you say you are.

> At Widget Tech, I captured the multi-million dollar win with Smith Systems, earning Smith's Supplier of the Year Award.

or

> I championed the use of SharePoint at Banyon Publishing and we saw a 50% improvement in division-wide efficiency and decision-making.

or

> ...that's how I brought Turtleneck Industries back to profitability within 6 months after narrowly avoiding an impending bankruptcy. Not only did I turn Turtleneck around,

the next five years brought us double-digit sales and profit growth.

Tell Your Reader What to Do

Now let's give your reader a clear call to action.

A clear call to action tells your reader what to do once they have finished reading your profile. It is an instruction of what they should do and an explanation of what they can expect in return.

Why is this important? The last thing you want is your reader to surf away and forget all about you.

In order to have a clear call to action, determine how your reader should get in contact with you. You have a number of options:

- Visit my Website
- Send me an email
- Call me
- Connect with me on LinkedIn®

If you have privacy concerns, your best bet is to either direct your reader to a Website or ask them to connect with you on LinkedIn®. By providing your email or phone number in your summary, it is available to not just the people in your network but potentially any Sam, Dick, or Harry outside your network. Remember, it is called your *public* profile for a reason.

My recommendation is to include a telephone number or email address. You are on LinkedIn® to network and find business opportunities. Providing contact information on your profile allows people to contact you outside the confines of LinkedIn®.

By trying to avoid the occasional telemarketer, you may also be avoiding real opportunity. The movers and shakers of this world are direct people and they want to contact you immediately. If they can't find your phone number, they may move on to the next person.

Once you have your contact method chosen, let's close the sale and ask for the check.

> I am currently looking for that next position that will allow me to simplify processes, affect change, and improve the bottom line.
>
> Please check out my resume on my Website, mywebsite.com and then connect with me on LinkedIn® to set up a time to talk further.

> or

> An email is all it takes to see if you are a candidate for my services. Whether you are struggling with malfunctioning printers or spending too much money on expensive ink cartridges, give me a call.
>
> Let's get your printing services running efficiently.
>
> Email me at gmail@gmail.com

Another way of crafting this call to action is tempting them with a carrot. Give your reader a reason to get in touch with you. Will you provide them with a free phone consultation? Do you have experience that you are open to sharing?

Here are some examples:

> Call me today for a free phone consultation to see if your business can benefit from my services. Let's put the proper solutions into action and together we'll turn your goals into reality.

> or

I'd love to share with you some of the insights I've gleaned from managing and measuring the effectiveness of Websites over the last 10 years.

Let's talk! My number is: (555) 666-7777

If you are a reputation seeker, a call to action may not be necessary. Determine what is appropriate for you. You may decide to end on a high note.

A high note ending is when you gently end your narrative in a positive way, leaving your reader feeling inspired.

Here are a few examples:

My success is my clients' success. I gain genuine satisfaction from helping non-profit organizations optimize their fundraising efforts. Knowing that I have helped not only the non-profit but the people they help is what keeps me striving forward.

or

The bottom line is I help my clients save money and plan for a secure future.

or

My focus moving forward is to continue to grow revenue and affect positive change within this amazing organization.

The Importance of Formatting

Powerful LinkedIn® profiles have paragraph breaks. Click the enter/return key on your keyboard to put space between the paragraph sections of your summary. This goes for all job descriptions, too. You want to make it easy for your reader to read the content. Spaces between paragraphs help.

Summary Example #1

Do you have a home to sell in New York City? Or maybe you are looking to move to New York City?

Are you in need of a real estate agent who will patiently and kindly walk you through the home buying/selling process?

My name is Deanna Cage and as a realtor, I help individuals and families in New York City through the home buying and selling process.

I have a strong background in sales which is the reason why I have consistently been able to sell higher-end and hard to sell homes in the current economic market.

I work equally well with senior home buyers and first time home buyers that require more time and education in the real estate process.

My strong Web presence allows for my real estate listings to be seen worldwide. I am able to bring prospective home buyers in from areas far outside the local New York City area.

So what are you waiting for? Let's find you the house of your dreams today. Give me a call. 555-555-1234.

Summary Example #2

Could your business use a faster responding, more reliable and more experienced IT support staff?

Look no further. My name is Micky Presley and I help small business owners reduce technology costs, communicate better with their clients and become more efficient with their time and money.

The fortune 500 companies spend huge sums of money on large IT departments. Here's the thing: Smaller companies need the same support mechanisms, just on a smaller scale. And believe it or not, this type of support is not outside a small business's price range. You see, that's where I come in.

I have been working in the IT industry for over 13 years and have consulted for some of the largest organizations in the Boston region, such as Copper, Trackside, and many others.

Every solution that I bring to the table has my philosophy of Reliability, Security, and Scalability built into it.

I only use tried and true, industry-proven solutions. I truly partner with my clients and my goal is to become an integral part of their organization.

You don't need someone who just fixes problems. You need an IT Consultant who provides unique solutions that help your small business communicate better and run more efficiently.

Visit my Website for more information on my services:

http://www. Roselein-IT.com

Summary Example #3

My name is Nigel Davies and I am an eagle-eyed CPA with an MBA.

I've spent the last 8 years working in the very hectic world of IRS Auditing. I became quite adept at spotting even the slightest inconsistency. Juggling multiple projects, regardless of their pressing deadlines, became a normal part of my day. In fact, I thrive on fast-paced projects.

I've found that one of my most admired skills is the ability to see the big picture and how the different parts of the whole process work together. This ability allows me to spot simple solutions to complex issues.

The good news is I am currently looking for that next position that will allow me to simplify processes, affect change, and improve the bottom line.

If your organization is looking for a CPA who has a strong business background AND who can transform business processes, we should talk.

Connect with me on LinkedIn® and let's arrange a time to speak.

Summary Example #4

My name is Matthew Simone and I am a Construction Manager with a diverse history in the building industry. I've spent the last 3 decades in a variety of roles ranging from Construction Carpenter to Sales, Operations Manager to Site Manager, to where I am today, working with the leading Home Builder in the San Diego area, Magellan Homes.

I pride myself on the reputation I've built constructing quality projects in an expedient and profitable manner.

My reputation comes from my knowledge of the building trades: electrical, plumbing, roofing, siding, flooring, HVAC, and carpentry.

One of the reasons I got into construction was that I thrive on high pressure work environments and can multitask easily. In fact, I've been able to successfully juggle 5 construction projects simultaneously while completing a total of 100 construction projects annually.

Ultimately, I take the lead and get construction projects done... on time and under budget.

If you have any questions or would like to discuss my construction experience, please connect with me on LinkedIn®. I am always looking to network with like-minded individuals but I am not an open networker, so please refer to your opportunity in your request to connect.

5

Contact Information

Phone ★ Address ★ IM
Twitter ★ Status Updates

Contact Information

The Contact Information section is located directly above your summary. Consider this section your digital business card in your network's LinkedIn® rolodex. Oddly enough, this section is often left blank which I find truly puzzling. If you don't fill out your contact information, how will opportunity know where to knock?

Let's fill it out

1.   From the Edit Profile page, click Edit Contact Information.
2.   The Contact Information section will appear.

In the Telephone Number field, enter your home, work, or mobile telephone number. The next field is IM. IM stands for instant messenger. Instant messenger is a way to send and receive short text-based messages instantly either by phone or by using a chat client on your computer. The instant messenger types that LinkedIn® accepts are:

- AIM (AOL)
- Skype
- Windows Live Messenger
- Yahoo! Messenger
- ICQ
- GTalk (Gmail)

Choose the IM you use most often and enter your username in the field provided. If you don't IM, leave the field blank. Here's the thing, you can only choose one IM. If you use more than 1 instant messenger service, determine what service is most used by your target audience and choose that one.

Skype is a great IM to add. Not only is it free but many organizations use Skype for video calls. In fact, Skype is often an integral part of the hiring process. Skype is used for on the fly job interviews. By including a Skype username, you are showing that you are easily available to them and that they don't need to spend time getting you up and running on it. That's definitely a bonus for a busy recruiter or HR professional.

If you don't have a Skype account, don't worry. It's easy to register. Simply visit, Skype.com and register for a free account.

The Address field is for your work or office address. If you work from home and are not comfortable including your home address, at least enter your city, state and zip. This way people will know where you are generally located.

Why do so many people leave this section blank? I think people are hesitant to fill out this section because they're afraid of being targeted by telemarketers and psychopaths. Here's the thing, only people who are connected to you directly will be able to see it. So if you are scared of telemarketers and psychopaths, don't connect with them!

If you are absolutely against putting your contact information out there, you can choose to ignore this section. I must caution you against omitting your contact information. LinkedIn® is all about connections and if you won't let your network communicate with you, how can you truly connect?

Success on LinkedIn® is getting off LinkedIn®. The movers and shakers in this world aren't satisfied sending an email and waiting for a response. When they want to talk, they want to pick up the phone and talk. Make it easy for them to contact you. Remember, strong relationships are shaped in the real world. Don't be afraid to leave the digital comfort of LinkedIn® for real world connection. That's where success truly resides.

Website

LinkedIn® provides you with 3 backlinks to your Website and/or blog. Backlinks are very important in the world of SEO. Search engines give more authority and higher rank to sites that have incoming links. You see, backlinks are considered the leading indicator of the importance of a Website. The more backlinks you have, the higher you will rank in the eyes of a search engine.

In fact, it's not just the number of backlinks to your Website that affect SEO rankings. It's also important that the sites that link to your Website are highly ranked in search engine results. LinkedIn® is a highly regarded site so backlinks from LinkedIn® are valued even more highly than a link from a little po-dunk site like Bob's Home Page. It's possible to outrank a site with more backlinks simply by getting a few links from well-regarded, highly ranked Websites.

Anchor text is also very important when it comes to search engine optimization. Anchor text is the hyperlinked words on a Web page. These are the underlined words you click that link you to another Website.

Hyperlinked words mean the world to a search engine. You see, search engines use that anchor text in their ranking algorithms. The anchor text tells the search engine what the linked page is about and the search engine ranking for those keywords will increase.

Enough of this lesson on search engine optimization, let's get back to LinkedIn®.

LinkedIn® provides you with two fields for your Website. The first field is a drop list for the anchor text and the other is a text field to enter the Website's URL. The drop list choices are:

- Personal Website
- Company Website
- Blog
- RSS Feed
- Portfolio
- Other

Most people choose either, Personal Website, Company Website or Blog. But not you! You are going to buck this trend, my friend.

Choose Other. Why Other? Well, by choosing Other, you are able to choose your own anchor text.

You could choose from LinkedIn®'s drop list, but who would search for those terms? No one! Instead of accepting the default choices, determine the keywords a person might use if they are searching for your Website. Use these search terms as your anchor text.

Do you want to be found by your name? Perhaps you want to be found by your company name? Rather than going the direct route, maybe you want to be found for the keywords that describe your services or skills:

- Real Estate Agent Delaware
- Business Intelligence Analyst
- Website Design Ohio

You only have 30 characters available for anchor text so you must be brief.

If you are listing the Website for a company that you do not own or manage, you may not care about the SEO of the LinkedIn®

backlink. Regardless, I don't recommend choosing, My Company from the drop list. Instead, choose Other and in the anchor text field, type in the name of your company. By entering the company name, you are helping your reader identify the link easily.

This is how your Website section should look:

Other	Donna Serdula Bio	http://www.DonnaSerdula.com/bio
Other	Public Speaker	http://www.DonnaSerdula.com
Other	Profile Writer	http://www.LinkedIn-Makeover.com

These backlinks are golden since they are coming from LinkedIn®. Don't waste this opportunity.

Contact Information Example

Email: donna@gmail.com

IM: donna.serdula (Skype)

Twitter: donnaserdula

Phone: 215-839-0008 (work)

Address: Vision Board Media
1 Elm Street
Suite 101
Philadelphia, PA 18967

Websites:

OTHER LinkedIn® Profile Writer   http://www.LinkedIn-Makeover.com

OTHER Keynote Speaker   http://www.DonnaSerdula.com

OTHER Vision Board Media   http://www.VIBoMe.com/

Twitter

Did you know that you can link your LinkedIn® account to Twitter?

By linking your Twitter account with your LinkedIn® profile, you are able to kill two birds with one stone. When you post a LinkedIn® status update about your day and accomplishments, you can have that status message go to both LinkedIn® and Twitter.

In order to set up this cross-posting (LinkedIn® to Twitter) ability, you must have a Twitter account.

Linking Your Twitter account to LinkedIn®

1. Click Profile > Edit Profile on LinkedIn®'s top navigation bar.
2. Click Edit Contact Information.
3. Click the edit icon to the right of the word Twitter and in the resulting pop up window, click +Add link to add your Twitter Account.
4. A Twitter window will pop up asking you to approve the account link.

Once this link is in place, you will see a little Twitter checkbox next to your LinkedIn® status update field. By clicking on the Twitter checkbox, your LinkedIn® status update will be cross-posted to LinkedIn®'s network activity and Twitter.

But I Don't Tweet

You don't tweet? Don't you know it's the 21st Century and everyone is supposed to share what they had for lunch with the world via Twitter? I tease, but there are professional reasons to join Twitter.

Are you a person who wants to market and brand yourself online? Do you want to tell the world you are an expert in your chosen field? Signing up for Twitter and then sharing your LinkedIn® status updates with your Twitter followers is a great way to promote yourself as an expert.

I know what you are thinking, "How does tweeting what I had for dinner impress people?"

It doesn't. But tweeting your knowledge, providing advice, directing people to interesting articles and adding value does.

Here's the thing, don't feel bullied into using Twitter. Twitter is great for some people but it's not necessary for everyone. Use your best judgment when deciding to sign up for Twitter. If you can't see yourself posting regularly, don't even bother. The worst thing is a Twitter page that is dormant.

LinkedIn® Status Updates

Before we get too far ahead of ourselves introducing Twitter into the mix, you must remember that LinkedIn® is a social networking site. Like most social networking sites, LinkedIn® gives you the opportunity to broadcast status updates to your connections. These messages are sent as a network update to your connections and are posted on the LinkedIn® home page under All Updates.

Status updates are a great way of sharing small bursts of information with your LinkedIn® connections. You can send out an update letting people know you posted a new blog entry, that you have a speaking engagement coming up, or that you found an article on the Web interesting. You can also provide advice, offer a quote of inspiration, announce something newsworthy about your company, or talk about recent results of a project or work activity.

Do not share updates about your child's soccer team win or pictures of cute kittens. LinkedIn® is a professional social network so save the personal stuff for Facebook or Twitter.

LinkedIn® status updates are a great way to communicate with your connections without using email. Not only should you post status updates but you should keep an eye on the status updates of your connections. To get to this area, just scroll down your LinkedIn® home page. Status updates appear right below the LinkedIn® Today section.

Think of LinkedIn®'s home page as your own, personalized newspaper. All the articles are provided by people you know and the news is tailored specifically for you. In fact, under each article is an op ed section where you can immediately provide feedback and converse with the person who shared the article with you.

By reading the status updates of your connections, you are keeping abreast of what they are doing. When you comment on a status update, you are letting that person know that you take an interest in their lives. This comment is then broadcast out and all their connections can see it. You may actually find yourself having a conversation in the comments section of a LinkedIn® status update with people outside your network.

It's important to not just use LinkedIn® as a soapbox but rather use it for dialog. You want to post statuses that engage people. Statuses that have comments are successful statuses. The easiest way to get people to start commenting on your statuses is by making sure you are commenting on theirs. When people see you are interested in them, they can't help but get interested in you. The more comments on your status updates, the more buzz you receive and the more people hear about you. What are you waiting for? Get out there and start interacting with your connections.

How Do I Post a Status Update?

You can post a status update straight from your LinkedIn® home page.

1. Click Home on the top of LinkedIn®'s navigation bar.
2. At the top of the home page near your profile photo is the posting module. Click into the text box and type in your status update. You are limited to 600 characters maximum.
3. You can also paste a Web address into this area. LinkedIn will recognize the URL and a title, description and thumbnail image will automatically display.
4. Clicking on the automatically generated title and description will allow you to edit them. If a thumbnail image was added, you may be able to click the arrow to choose a different image.
5. You can also click the paperclip icon to attach a document to your status.
6. If you have a Twitter account authenticated with your LinkedIn® account, you can choose to cross post your status update on LinkedIn® only or LinkedIn® and Twitter. Only the first 140 characters of your status update will show on Twitter. This is also where you can choose if the status update is seen only by your connections or all LinkedIn® members.
7. Click Share.

Your status is now viewable by your network. If anyone likes, comments on, or shares it with their network, you will receive a notification that activity occurred. This notification appears under the flag icon located on LinkedIn's top navigation bar.

4

Basic Information

Location & Industry
Name ★ Headline

Basic Information

You are close to the end! There's light at the end of the tunnel. Just a little further. Stay with me.

Basic Information is the section where you enter your location & industry, professional headline, and full name.

Location & Industry

The Location & Industry fields tell the world where you are located in this world and your industry.

Editing Location & Industry

1. Click Profile > Edit Profile on LinkedIn®'s top navigation bar.
2. Click the edit icon next to the city/area that is located at the top of your profile.

In order to show up in local LinkedIn® searches, you must fill out the Location and Industry fields with the correct information.

Location & Industry Example

Country
United States

Postal Code
18966

Location Name
○ Southampton, Pennsylvania
● Greater Philadelphia Area

Industry
Marketing & Advertising

Take a moment and pay close attention to the Industry drop list. Really peruse it and make sure to tag yourself correctly. I can't tell you how many profiles I have seen tagged with the incorrect industry or location.

The reason these fields need to be accurate is they are used to filter results in LinkedIn®'s advanced search.

Performing an Advanced Search

1.   Click the Advanced link located next to the search box on LinkedIn®'s top navigation bar.
2.   The advanced search page appears.
3.   Enter your search terms in the applicable fields and click Search.

Notice you can filter the search results by a selected geographic area or industry on the advanced search page. This information is pulled directly from your Location & Industry field of your profile.

Your Professional Headline

Your LinkedIn® headline is the shortened version of your profile. It tells who you are in 120 characters or less. The headline shows up right underneath your name on the top of your profile. Your headline is extremely important. It is your readers' very first impression of you and it will determine whether they continue reading or click to the next profile. Let's make sure your headline sings.

Editing Your Headline

1.   Click Profile > Edit Profile on LinkedIn®'s top navigation bar.

2.   Click the edit icon next to your headline at the very top of your profile.

Your headline sums up your professional identity in a very short phrase. You want this phrase to be catchy, bright and clever.

LinkedIn® automatically takes your current job title and uses it as your headline. Please do not accept this automatic headline. I assure you it is boring and compels no one to click your profile and learn more about you.

Why is the headline so important? The headline is visible on LinkedIn® search results, invitations to connect, and LinkedIn® messages. Since so many people see it, you want to make sure it absolutely communicates your value and compels people to open your profile to learn more about you.

Not all headlines are created equal. I have found there are 3 distinct headline types: the blah headline, power statement headline, and keyword-packed headline. Which one is right for you?

Blah Headline

The blah headline is nothing more than the person's job title and company. This is the headline LinkedIn® provides if you do not override the system default. It is awful and should be avoided at all cost.

> Account Manager at ABC Widget Co.

Power Statement Headline

The power statement headline is my personal favorite because if done well, it really tells a story and compels people to check out your profile.

> Social Media Consultant ▶ Helping businesses embrace social media and GROW!

When crafting a power statement headline, start with: Helping people... or Helping companies... and then just fill in the rest. The question to ask yourself is *how do you help people or companies achieve results?*

The next page contains a list of power statement headlines that you can use for inspiration.

Power Statement Headline Examples

Business Broker ▶ Helping Individuals Achieve Independence by Finding them the Business of Their Dreams

Business Analyst ▶ Helping Companies Translate Their Business Goals and Ideas to Operational Reality and Positive ROI

Sales Consultant ▶Helping Businesses Develop Strong Sales Forces through Intensive Sales Training Programs

Financial Coach ★ Helping People Overcome Challenges They Cannot Solve Themselves ★ How Can I Help You?

Software Engineer ▶ Building the Applications that Make Your Business Life Easier

Insurance Broker & Agent ▶ Protecting Families and Businesses in Ohio by Providing Expert Insurance Advice

Business Advisor ▶ Helping Manufacturing Facilities Realize Significant Gains through Process Improvement

Interim CEO ▶ Solving urgent leadership problems... when your CEO steps down, I step up!

Project Manager with a Passion for Coding and Technical Writing, Looking to Positively Impact a New Organization

IT Specialist Devoted To Creating Stable, Scalable Solutions for Small Businesses

New York's #1 Small Business Growth Coach helping Owners Retire to Tahiti

Keyword-Packed Headline

The keyword-packed headline is the most popular headline choice amongst LinkedIn® users. A keyword-packed headline is a great way to further optimize your profile because it uses your main keywords. When crafted in the right way, it can pack a punch.

Keyword-Packed Headline Examples

Holistic Health Coach ★ Foodie ★ World Traveler ★ Recovering Corporate Executive ★ Engaging Speaker ★ Pilates Addict

HR Consultant - Talent Development - Psychologist - Life Coach – Bayliner Captain

Planning & Strategies Consultant | Speaker |Trainer |Author

Solutions Oriented Sales ▶ Relationship Builder ▶ Strategizer ▶ Scrapbooker Extraordinaire

Leader, Winner, Game Changer, Entrepreneur, Humanitarian

Chief Executive Officer ● Turnaround Management Expert ● Business Development Champion ● Engaging Keynote Speaker

Real Estate Professional * Home Sales & Leasing Specialist * New Home Champion * Theater Buff

Engineering Executive ★ Plant Operations ★ Six Sigma Black Belt ★ English/French Fluent ★Strategic Leader

The real secret to the keyword-packed headline is coupling professional keywords with some personal, extracurricular ones.

Notice that many of these headlines mention being a sports fanatic or yoga addict? This turns the corporate creature into a three dimensional human being.

If you are job seeker, it's important you add your job title to your headline. Your headline is extremely sensitive when it comes to search engine optimization. Many recruiters and hiring managers, when performing searches for talent, will search for job titles. Make sure you include your title so you increase the chances of being found on LinkedIn®.

Remember those bullets from the job title section? Use your chosen bullet to separate your headline keywords.

Are you finding it difficult brainstorming an interesting headline? The next page contains my famous LinkedIn® Headline Generator. Using this wizard, you will have a sexy, compelling, LinkedIn® headline in less than five minutes flat. What are you waiting for? Turn the page to begin!

LinkedIn® Keyword Headline Generator

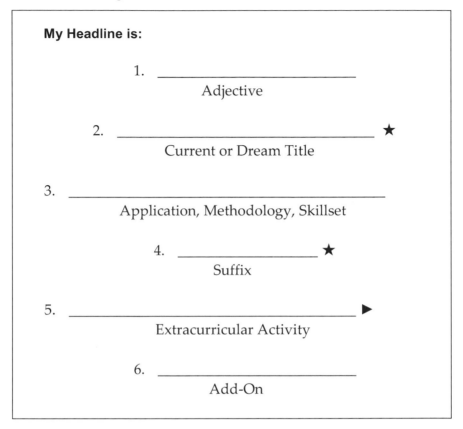

My Headline is:

1. _____
   Adjective

2. _____ ★
   Current or Dream Title

3. _____
   Application, Methodology, Skillset

4. _____ ★
   Suffix

5. _____ ▶
   Extracurricular Activity

6. _____
   Add-On

YOU ONLY HAVE 120 CHARACTERS SO CHOOSE WISELY!!!!

1. Start with an adjective

❐ Accomplished	❐ Experienced	❐ Effective	❐ Holistic
❐ Animated	❐ Executive	❐ Dynamic	❐ Freelance
❐ Certified	❐ Energetic	❐ Expert	❐ Itinerant
❐ Engaging	❐ Influential	❐ Skilled	❐ Sassy
❐ Exciting	❐ Professional	❐ Masterful	❐ Capable
❐ Gifted	❐ Positive	❐ Innovative	❐ Unabashed

2. Add Your Current or Dream Role/Position

- ❏ CIO/CEO
- ❏ Sales Professional
- ❏ Writer
- ❏ Tech Consultant

- ❏ Human Resources Manager
- ❏ Account Manager

- ❏ Marketing Manager
- ❏ Speaker
- ❏ Project Manager

- ❏ Customer Service
- ❏ Corporate Executive
- ❏ Other:

Add a Bullet

● ✔ ★ ☞ ▶ · ☼ ☺ ●◊♦◻♫∎▪·—◻

Copy & Paste the bullet from here:
http://www.LinkedIn.com/in/todonna

3. Add either an Application or a Methodology or a Skillset

- ❏ PowerPoint
- ❏ Salesforce
- ❏ CRM

- ❏ Social Media
- ❏ CRM
- ❏ Business Development

- ❏ Personal Branding
- ❏ C++
- ❏ Marketing

- ❏ Leadership
- ❏ Other:

4. Add a Suffix

- ❏ Addict
- ❏ Advisor
- ❏ Advocate
- ❏ Aficionado
- ❏ Artist
- ❏ Builder

- ❏ Catalyst
- ❏ Champion
- ❏ Coach
- ❏ Crusader
- ❏ Curator
- ❏ Developer

- ❏ Enthusiast
- ❏ Expert
- ❏ Extraordinaire
- ❏ Fanatic
- ❏ Generator
- ❏ Guru

- ❏ Lover
- ❏ Maven
- ❏ Maestro
- ❏ Optimizer
- ❏ Specialist
- ❏ Strategizer

Add a Bullet

● ✔ ★ ☞ ▶ · ☼ ☺ ●◊♦◻♫∎▪·—◻

5. Add an Extracurricular Activity

❏ Foodie
❏ Marathon Runner
❏ Humanitarian
❏ Golfer

❏ Community Organizer
❏ Pilates Star
❏ Sports Fanatic

❏ Geek
❏ Tech Whiz
❏ Health Fanatic
❏ Volunteer

❏ World Traveler
❏ Yoga Addict
❏ Other:

Add a Bullet

● ✔ ★ ☞ ▶ • ☼ ☺ ● ◊ ♦ ◻ ♫ ■ ▪ — ▫

6. Add an Add-on

❏ Change Agent
❏ Thought Leader
❏ Corporate Athlete
❏ Powerhouse
❏ Best in Breed
❏ Gifted

❏ Brand Evangelist
❏ Enlightened Leader
❏ Game Changer
❏ Corporate Player/Pawn

❏ Read My Profile!
❏ Click to Learn More!

❏ Curious? Read on...
❏ Click Here!
❏ LION
❏ Rock On

For more Headline examples and instructions please visit:
http://www.LinkedIn-Makeover.com/linkedIn-headline-generator

Your Name

The Name field should be the easiest field to fill out but some people find it confusing, especially if they are known by a nickname.

Editing Your Name

1.   Click Profile > Edit Profile on LinkedIn®'s top navigation bar.
2.   Click the edit icon next to your name at the very top of your profile.

If you are an employment seeker and your name is Stanislav but everyone calls you Stan - but your resume says Stanislav -- go with Stanislav. If you are a business seeker or a reputation seeker and your name is Stanislav but everyone calls you Stan - and your business cards say Stan -- go with Stan.

The key is to make it easy for people to find you by being consistent with your name.

Do you see the Former Name field? This field is for former names, maiden names or nicknames. It displays on your LinkedIn® profile encased in parenthesis between your first and last name. It does not display on your public profile. This means that if a person performs a search using your former name on Google or Bing, your profile will not turn up in the search results; however if a person searches within LinkedIn®, you will be found.

But I want to be Anonymous

There is an option that allows you to include only your last initial on your LinkedIn® profile. In order to access this option, you must turn off your public profile. Once your public profile is turned off, the option to display your name with only your last initial appears within your Name field. If you live in a log cabin off grid and are truly protective of your privacy, displaying just your last initial may be a good idea. Most people use LinkedIn® to network and connect with people and business opportunities. Displaying your full name shows you are serious in these goals. Unless you are using LinkedIn® under confidential circumstances, my recommendation is to display your full name.

3

Public Profile Settings

Customize Your Public Profile ★ Profile Review & Checklist
Claiming Your Public URL

Public Profile

The Public Profile section is where you preview your profile and set the public viewing options for your profile. You determine what profile sections people outside of your network can view. This area is also where you can customize your profile's Web address by claiming an easy to use URL for marketing purposes.

Previewing Your Public Profile

1.   From the Edit Profile page, click the Edit link to the right of your public profile URL.
2.   The Public Profile page appears.

Customize Your Public Profile

The Public Profile page shows you a preview of what non-LinkedIn® users and LinkedIn® members outside your network see when they visit your LinkedIn® profile.

To the right of the public profile preview is a box entitled, Customize Your Public Profile. This is where you choose to either turn off your public profile entirely or disable certain profile sections.

Your public profile preview area updates as you uncheck profile content. Determine what profile content you want to display to those people outside your LinkedIn® network.

Employment seekers and reputation seekers should keep every section of their public profile turned on because according to their goals, they want readers to learn more about them. Business seekers may opt to turn off the details of their past positions if their previous positions hold little value to their potential clients.

Claiming Your Public URL

LinkedIn® automatically assigns your profile a default Web address. The default address is quite ugly. A jumble of letters and numbers that is not easy to remember or market. But that's okay. LinkedIn® gives you the ability to change this URL to something easy to remember and easy to promote.

What's more easy to remember than your name? By choosing your name, you are claiming ownership of your profile. Whatever you do, do not use your company's name as your public URL. Your public URL is a permanent link to your LinkedIn® profile. Companies, on the other hand, do not always have permanence in your life

Setting Your LinkedIn® Public URL

1.   From the Edit Profile page, click the Edit link to the right of your public profile URL.
2.   Your public profile appears.
3.   In the column to the right of your public profile is a box entitled, Your public profile URL.
4.   Click the link, Customize your public profile URL.
5.   In the field provided, enter your new URL. I suggest using your name.
6.   Click the Set Custom URL button.

My Name Is Not Available

Is your name already taken? It happens. Let's find an alternative way of stating your name.

Pretend your name is John Smith. Here are some ideas of re-phrasing your name that might not yet be taken:

• First initial and last name: JSmith
• First name, middle initial and last name: JohnASmith

- First and middle initial and last name: JASmith
- Add the word "to" in front of first and last name: ToJohnSmith (get it? Linked in to John Smith)

I often see people add numbers to the end of their name. I highly discourage adding numbers. In the immortal words of Patrick McGoohan from the iconic television series, The Prisoner, "I am not a number. I am a free man!" Rather than showing your lower rank, find a creative way of stating your name to show your uniqueness.

A customized, public URL looks like this:

http://www.LinkedIncom/in/VanityName

Include your LinkedIn® public URL on:

- Business Cards
- Resume
- Email Signature
- Website
- Brochures
- Sales Literature
- Letterhead

By claiming your public URL, not only does it provide you with potentially better SEO, but more importantly, it is easy to remember and easy to market.

2

Profile Photo

Profile Photo ★ Why Add a Photo?
Uploading a Photo

Profile Photo

Say cheese! It's time to upload a picture.

Why Add a Photo?

According to LinkedIn® research, profiles with a profile picture are seven times more likely to be viewed than profiles without a profile picture. That's a big difference. Simply uploading a picture proves you are a serious LinkedIn® user and networker and someone who deserves respect. A professional photo shows your reader that there is a real person behind the profile.

Profile photos are not just relegated to your profile. Your profile photo acts as an eye catching bullet to your name. When your profile appears in search results, your smiling mug peers out from next to your name and subliminally implores your reader to, Read all about me!" Profile photos also appear along with your group messages, status updates, recommendations, and endorsements.

People are impressed by the artificial. Instead of teaching the world a lesson, let's just play the game, post a picture, and in turn get more views to your profile.

Uploading a Photo

Do you have a nice picture of yourself? Is it in JPG, GIF or PNG file format? The size of the image should be a minimum of 200 by 200 pixels and a maximum of 500 by 500 pixels (File size limit is 4 MB). If you need to resize your image, you can do it in Microsoft Paint.

Let's get this picture uploaded.

1. From the Edit Profile page, locate either your current profile picture or the silhouetted image LinkedIn® uses as a space holder.
2. Click the camera icon on this silhouetted image. You are now at the Photo Upload page.
3. Click Choose File/Browse.
4. A window will open where you can select your photo from your hard drive. Find your photo and click Open.
5. Click Upload Photo to upload your image to LinkedIn®.

In much the same way Willy Wonka transported little Mike TeeVee, your image is magically transferred to LinkedIn®'s magic server cloud. Yes, that is the technical term.

Once uploaded, LinkedIn® displays a preview of your photo as others will see it. How does it look? Is your photo not centered correctly? Are your shoulders taking up too much screen real estate? Don't worry about it! Do you see that yellow dotted square atop your photo? You can resize that square so it fits your face. LinkedIn® will crop your photo along that yellow dotted line. When you are happy with your photo, click Save Photo.

I can't stress enough the need to ZOOM IN! You want your face to fill as much of the image as possible. The closer you appear to your reader, the closer they feel to you.

Choosing the Right Photo

No matter how tempting it might be, do not upload just any photo. You want to choose a picture that casts you in the best light. I don't mean one that just makes you look glamorous or sexy. The photo you choose should make you look professional.

In order to appear professional, consider using a photograph of yourself wearing a business suit, dress or at the very least, a business casual outfit. No bathing suits, t-shirts, bare chests, glaring expressions, logos, cartoon characters, etc...

I am reminded of something my mother once told me when I was starting out in my career, "Don't dress for the job you have, Donna, dress for the job you want!" If your office environment is a casual one, you still may decide to opt for a more formal business picture. Especially if you have higher aspirations for your career.

And smile. So many people seem to forget to smile in their photo and their excuse is they want to appear serious. That's all fine and dandy but more often than not, serious actually appears angry. No one wants to network with an angry person, so smile and look approachable.

What else? A professional photo is cropped and centered. A good professional photo is not too dark, grainy or taken from afar. There should only be one person in it... you. It's also important that the photo is current.

Recently, I met a man at a networking event and we agreed to connect on LinkedIn®. That night I located his profile but could not believe his profile picture. The man I met was a distinguished looking gentleman with gray hair and plenty of wrinkles but the man in this picture had dark hair and long sideburns. He may have felt 25 on the inside but choosing to post a photo of himself at 25 made him look foolish.

If your profile photo is older than two years, it's time to get a new one taken. The best tip I can offer is to go to a professional photographer. Looking your best is worth the investment. You have spent time making sure your profile is well-written and powerful, now you should complete it with a fantastic photograph of yourself.

It's hard for busy professionals to find the time to schedule a session with a photographer but it's something you need to make time to do. As tempting as it might be to ask them to come to your office, resist that urge. Go to their studio where they have professional lighting and backgrounds. The background you want to pick is a simple one. Choose a white or pale color background. Although I have seen dark backgrounds look good, the nicest LinkedIn® profile pictures are those with a pale/blank background. The idea is that you are the focus of the portrait, not a busy background.

When you are at the studio, make sure the camera is at eye level. You don't want to look up or down at the camera. Make eye contact. Don't look away. In your mind I want you to think: confident, friendly, well-adjusted.

Make sure you get lots of pictures taken. It often takes hundreds of shots to finally find one that is usable. Don't feel bad. You are a professional, not a super model. Bring a friend along who can help you choose the final picture.

The final picture should convey a person who is friendly, approachable, well-adjusted, and professional.

Do I Need A New Profile Picture?

Still not sure if you need to take a new LinkedIn® profile picture? On the next page there is a quiz to help you determine whether you are a candidate for a new profile picture. Answer either yes or no. There are no maybes.

LinkedIn® Profile Picture Quiz

Yes No

☐ ☐ Is your profile picture over 2 years old?

☐ ☐ Was your profile picture snapped at a wedding or family gathering?

☐ ☐ Does your profile picture contain another person other than just yourself?

☐ ☐ Are there remnants of another person cropped out of your profile picture?

☐ ☐ Are there animals in your profile picture?

☐ ☐ Are you wearing a hat or sunglasses in your profile picture?

☐ ☐ Is your profile picture of a cartoon character, business logo, symbol or artistic representation?

☐ ☐ Can you easily discern the background of your profile photo?

☐ ☐ Are you looking up or down or away from the viewer? Are you not making eye contact?

☐ ☐ Is the quality of the image grainy or dark?

☐ ☐ Are you not smiling? Do you look menacing, unfriendly, bored, or dull?

☐ ☐ Are you wearing a t-shirt, bathing suit, or jeans in your profile picture?

☐ ☐ Can you see your elbows or knees in your profile picture?

☐ ☐ Did you have someone other than a professional photographer take your profile photo?

If you answered yes to any of the questions above, you need a new profile photo. Even if you answered no to all the questions above, you still may need a new profile photo.

LinkedIn® Profile Photo Guidelines

- Your LinkedIn® profile picture can be as large as 4MB in size and can be in the following file formats: JPG, GIF, and PNG.

- Make sure your photo is at least 200 x 200 pixels and a maximum limit of 500 x 500 pixels.

- Do not use an image of a cartoon, symbol, drawing, or any content other than an actual photograph of yourself.

- A photograph that is not a current image of you is considered inappropriate.

- Lastly, remember to smile.

1

The Final Bits

Rearrange Profile Sections ★ Applications
Embed Video on Your Profile ★ LinkedIn® Settings
Upgrading Your Account ★ Improving Your Results

The Final Bits

In this last chapter... wait, I mean first chapter, I am going to show you how to re-order the sections of your profile, embed video, images, audio recordings, or even documents into your profile and optimize your LinkedIn® settings for a richer LinkedIn® experience.

Let's go!

Rearrange Profile Sections

Did you know you can re-order the sections of your LinkedIn® profile? The sections can be dragged and dropped wherever you want them to appear on your profile.

1.   Click Profile > Edit Profile on LinkedIn®'s top navigation bar.
2.   Scroll to the section you want to move.
3.   Click the little icon to the right of the section name, the one that looks like two arrows pointing upward and downward.
4.   Hold down your mouse button on that icon. Drag and drop the section almost anywhere on your profile.

Here's the thing, however tempting it may be, I suggest keeping your profile as close to default as possible. By straying too far from the default, you may confuse your reader.

I remember I once logged into a client's LinkedIn® profile and I couldn't find his Summary section. "Could I be going insane?" I thought as I clicked back and forth between the Edit Profile and View Profile pages. Finally I found his Summary section at the very bottom of his profile. Let this be a lesson. If you are missing a section, it may just be out of order.

The Perfect Order of Profile Sections

Here's my recommendation for a perfectly ordered LinkedIn® profile:

1.   Summary
2.   Experiences
3.   Projects
4.   Publications
5.   Honors & Awards
6.   Patents
7.   Skills & Expertise
8.   Languages
9.   Organizations
10.   Volunteer Experience & Causes
11.   Certifications
12.   Courses
13.   Education
14.   Test Scores
15.   Additional Information

Certainly, you may choose to move sections higher or lower on your profile depending on how pertinent the sections are to your goals. If you want to be viewed as highly educated and you have the schooling to prove it, move your Education section up higher on your profile. If you barely graduated from high school and don't want to spotlight your education, move it to the bottom of your profile. If you are proud of the books and articles you wrote, move the Publications section below your summary. If you work with nonprofits and you are proud of your volunteer experiences, move up the Volunteer Experiences & Causes section.

Embedding Work Samples

A powerful profile is not complete without rich media. You can now include presentations, videos, images, audio, documents, portfolios, and more embedded directly into your LinkedIn® profile. You can embed these items into your Summary, Experiences, and Education sections.

Have you created some amazing presentations? Perhaps you'd like to share brochures, whitepapers or company documents on your LinkedIn® profile? Get an account on Slideshare, Prezi or Scribd to share your masterpieces with the world. Do you have video of yourself or about your services & products you'd like to showcase on your LinkedIn® profile? Upload the video to Youtube, Prezi, or Viddler to embed it on your LinkedIn® profile.

Adding Media Samples to Your Profile

1.   Click Profile > Edit Profile on LinkedIn®'s top navigation bar.
2.   Scroll down to the section you want to add a sample to and click the icon that looks like a square with a plus sign.

      Note: Not every LinkedIn® user has access to this functionality yet. If you don't see this icon on your profile, you just need to be patient.

3.   You have two options: Upload File or Add Link. Select Upload File to have LinkedIn® host the file on your profile OR select Add Link to link to content that exists on a 3rd party's Website.

      Upload a file: Simply select the file from your computer.

      Add a link: Type or paste the link to your content into the provided field.

4.   Click Save.

Your profile now has glorious rich media embedded within it, separating your profile from the legions of other profiles that only contain boring text. Look out Hollywood! There's a new star in heaven tonight.

Review Your Work

You just spent a lot of time and effort optimizing your LinkedIn® profile. It is now time to review your public profile and your full LinkedIn® profile. You want to make sure that you didn't miss any sections or make any mistakes.

Public Profile Review

Your public profile is your LinkedIn® profile's face to the world. This is how people who are not LinkedIn® members see your LinkedIn® profile. Let's make sure it looks good.

1.   Click Profile on LinkedIn®'s top navigation bar.
2.   Scroll down to your public profile URL and click it.
3.   Your public profile appears.

How does your public profile look? Does it shine? Are you filled with a sense of pride and accomplishment? Is the profile easy to read and interesting? Are there any typos?

Full Profile Review

Now it's time to see how your profile looks to your LinkedIn® network.

1.   Click Profile on LinkedIn®'s top navigation bar.
2.   Starting at the top, use the checklist on the next page to make sure your profile is customized and complete.

Let's make sure all the sections are customized completely. As you view your full profile, check off each completed section.

Profile Checklist

☐ **Profile Picture**

Is your profile picture professionally taken? Do you look warm, friendly, and well-adjusted? Is the background neutral and not distracting?

☐ **Name**

Is your name spelled correctly? Is it consistent with your business card, resume, etc?

☐ **Headline**

Is your headline interesting? Will it compel a person to want to learn more about you?

☐ **Location & Industry**

Is your location correct? Is your industry accurate?

☐ **Customized Public Profile URL**

Did you customize the link to your public URL?

☐ **Contact Information**

Did you include your phone number, email, and IM? Did you add links to your Websites and Twitter?

☐ **Summary**

Is your summary engaging and easy to read? Does it introduce you to your reader? Does it provide a clear call to action?

☐ **One current and two past Experiences**

Are your Experience Titles packed with keywords? Do the descriptions contain a boilerplate on the company along with your performance highlights?

☐ **Skills and Expertise**

Did you add your core strengths, skillsets, and abilities?

☐ **Education**

Did you list at least one education... even if you did not graduate?

☐ **Additional Profile Sections**
Did you add Honors & Awards, Organizations, Volunteer
Experience & Causes, Certifications, Languages, Projects,
Publications, Patents, Test Scores, and/or Courses? Are you
showcasing yourself as a well-rounded professional?

☐ **Additional Information**
Did you add your interests and advice for contacting you?

☐ **Recommendations**
Do you have glowing recommendations on your profile from people
in high places?

☐ **Connections**
Do you have at least fifty 1st degree connections?

☐ **Groups**
Did you join up to 50 LinkedIn® Groups that contain not only
your target audience but also large amounts of members?

☐ **Following Influencers, News, and Companies**
Are you following influencers and companies that interest
you? At least 5? Are you following news items that provide
you with information on your industry and interests?

Is there a checkmark next to each category? If so, then you've
completed your profile. Congratulations! I think a happy dance
is in order. It's okay, nobody is looking. Jig away. Before you get
too carried away, there are a few more items still left to
accomplish that will further enhance your LinkedIn®
experience. The next section will take you through your
LinkedIn® settings.

LinkedIn® Settings

LinkedIn® allows quite a bit of control over your LinkedIn® experience through the customization of your settings page. The default settings work just fine but there are a few tweaks that will enhance your experience.

Accessing LinkedIn®'s Settings

1. On the upper right-hand corner of your LinkedIn® page, hover your cursor over your photo.
2. A drop list will appear. Click Privacy and Settings.

We will not visit every setting on this page. Regardless, I do recommend that you explore the sections we don't cover on your own. There is quite a bit of customization available to you.

There are four sections on this page:

- Profile
- Communications
- Groups, Companies, & Applications
- Account

Profile

Click Profile to begin editing this section.

Turn on/off your activity broadcasts

When you make changes to your profile or update your status, LinkedIn® notifies your connections of these changes. You can turn off this alert so your network isn't bombarded with your profile updates. This is especially important if you don't want your current employer to see that you are editing your LinkedIn® profile.

By selecting this option, your activity updates will be shared in your activity feed.

☑ Let people know when you change your profile, make recommendations, or follow companies

You should have turned off your activity broadcasts when we began this journey together. Now that your profile is optimized, it's time to turn the broadcasts back on. Don't worry, all the changes you made won't be sent in bulk. Only changes made after turning on this option will get sent out as status updates.

Select who can see your activity feed

Your activity feed shows the actions you've performed on LinkedIn®. It is displayed underneath the top section of your profile and above your Summary section. It is only visible to others when they're signed in to LinkedIn® and does not appear on your public profile. In order to increase your visibility on LinkedIn®, make sure you are broadcasting your activity feed to everyone.

Your activity feed displays actions you've performed on LinkedIn®. Select who can see your activity feed.

☑ Everyone

☐ Your network

☐ Your connections

☐ Only you

Select what others see when you've viewed their profile

The more you use LinkedIn®, the more you will find yourself checking out other people's profiles. Did you know that depending on your settings, people may be able to see that you viewed their profile? If you want to be invisible as you lurk around LinkedIn®, make sure you select the option that reads, Nothing. I will be completely invisible to users I have viewed. Rather than being totally invisible, you may choose to provide anonymous profile characteristics of yourself. Selecting anonymous profile characteristics will allow people to see that Someone in [insert your chosen Industry] has viewed their profile.

When I view other LinkedIn® profiles, those users will see:

☑ Your name and headline (Recommended)

☐ Anonymous profile characteristics, such as industry and title. *(Note: Selecting this option will disable Profile Stats)*

☐ Nothing. You will be totally anonymous.
(Note: Selecting this option will disable Profile Stats)

LinkedIn® recommends identifying yourself to the owners of the profiles you view. This way the profile owner can in turn view your profile.

If you want to see who has viewed your profile, you must identify yourself when you check out their profile. Quid pro quo. If you are uninterested in seeing who has visited your LinkedIn® profile and you don't want people to know you are a LinkedIn® profile stalker, opt to show nothing.

There is no right or wrong way to fill this section out. It all depends on your preferences. Of course, if you ask me, my recommendation is to allow yourself to be seen. By opting to remain visible, not only can you see who's checking out your profile but you can also direct more people to your profile.

Most LinkedIn® users love to see who's checked out their profile and they visit that user's profile in return. By viewing people's profile, you are inviting them to visit yours. And since you took the time to optimize your profile, you are making sure people are learning more about you and possibly giving them a reason to call you.

Communications

Click Communications to begin editing this section.

Select the types of messages you're willing to receive

LinkedIn® provides the opportunity to connect with people inside and outside of your professional network. There are numerous ways within LinkedIn® a user might choose to contact you. You can select the types of messages you are willing to accept.

What type of messages will you accept?

MESSAGES

☑ Introductions, InMail & OpenLink messages (Premium Members)

☑ Introductions and InMail Only (Free Members)

☐ Introductions Only

OPPORTUNITIES

☑ Career opportunities   ☑ Expertise requests

☑ Consulting offers   ☑ Business deals

☑ New ventures ☑ Personal reference requests

☑ Job inquiries ☑ Requests to reconnect

Advice to people who are contacting you

I love to connect with people on LinkedIn® but I am a conservative open networker. If I don't know you personally, please include why you want to connect in your invitation. Thanks so much.

The question this page asks you is: What type of messages will you accept on LinkedIn? You can accept Introductions, InMail, or OpenLink messages. So what does *that* mean?

Introductions

Using LinkedIn®, you can see how people are connected to you. Does that VIP you are dying to meet know someone you know? If so, you may ask your mutual connection for an introduction.

Introductions allow you to contact users in your network, through the people you know. LinkedIn® allows you to request 5 Introductions with a free LinkedIn® account.

InMail

InMails are private messages you send to people outside your network. These are people with whom you share no common connections.

InMails are not available to people with the free LinkedIn® account. In order to send InMails, you must upgrade to a paid account.

OpenLink

Only premium LinkedIn® members have the option to join the OpenLink Network. This means anyone on LinkedIn® who is also part of the OpenLink Network can send you a message or job opportunity for free, without an introduction or InMail. People who opt into the OpenLink Network have the OpenLink icon next to their name. The OpenLink Network icon looks like a wreath of circles.

My recommendation is to accept either Introductions, InMail and OpenLink messages or Introductions and InMail, depending on whether you are a premium member or not. Choosing to accept all types of communication methods ensures you aren't excluding any potential opportunities that may be professionally valuable to you. On the other hand, if you are a very important person, constantly harassed by marketers and sycophants, you may want to disallow InMail. In order to get the full power of LinkedIn®, I suggest you choose to accept all types of messages.

Opportunities

LinkedIn® allows you to connect and communicate with other professionals on LinkedIn®. By connecting with people, you expose yourself to potential business opportunities. You can choose the types of opportunities you want to receive via LinkedIn®:

- Career Opportunities
- Consulting Offers
- New Ventures
- Job Inquiries

- Expertise Requests
- Business Deals
- Personal Reference Requests
- Request to Reconnect

What opportunities are you interested in receiving via LinkedIn®?

LinkedIn® Opportunity Definitions

Career Opportunities: Are you interested in finding new job opportunities?

Consulting Offers: Are you interested in working with another company doing freelance consulting work?

New Ventures: Are you open to investing in new business opportunities?

Job Inquiries: Is your company looking for new employees?

Expertise Requests: Do you want to share your expertise with others?

Business Deals: Are you interested in conducting new business on LinkedIn®?

Personal Reference Requests: Are you interested in providing former and current colleagues or employees with recommendations of their work?

Requests to Reconnect: Are you open to reconnecting with people from your past?

Place a checkmark next to each opportunity you are interested in receiving. It's okay to check off all the opportunity types.

The Career Opportunities Dilemma

People often ask me if it's okay to check off Career Opportunities, especially if they are happily employed and don't want to rock the boat.

Only you know your employer and if you sense they might vociferously object to your openness regarding career opportunities, then leave it off.

My opinion is that it's absolutely acceptable to check off Career Opportunities because whether you admit it or not, you are always looking for the next best career move. Most employers are well aware of this proclivity and in a way, isn't it a good thing that they know you are open to something better? Maybe then they'll treat you right, knowing they could lose you to a more lucrative opportunity?

Select who can send you invitations

LinkedIn® is all about networking and connecting. This setting allows you to determine who can send you invitations. If set incorrectly, this setting can make it very difficult for people to network and connect with you.

Who can send you invitations

☑ Anyone on LinkedIn® (Recommended)

☐ Only people who know my email address or appear in my "Imported Contacts" list.

☐ Only people who appear in my "Imported Contacts" list.

Unless you are a celebrity or in the public eye, you should select, Anyone on LinkedIn®. By choosing the middle option, when a person wants to connect with you, they are prompted to enter your email address to complete the sending of the invitation. This might not sound terrible but it is very annoying being forced to find a person's email address just to connect with them. Most people cancel out and move on without connecting.

One of my clients once told me he rarely gets requests to connect on LinkedIn®. It seemed very odd since this was a person who was very involved in his community and a business leader. When I went to add him to my network, I was prompted to enter his email address. Clearly this was the reason why people were not connecting. No one had the time to search for his email address to enter it into LinkedIn®. Once we changed this setting to accept all invitations, he suddenly started receiving invitations to connect and he was able to grow his network.

Do yourself a favor and make it easy on people. Choose to accept invitations from anyone on LinkedIn®.

Groups, Companies & Applications

Click Groups, Companies & Applications to edit this section.

Set the frequency of group digest emails

If you followed my directions exactly, you should have joined 50 LinkedIn® Groups. You may now find that your email inbox is getting clogged with LinkedIn® Group emails. If this is the case, turn off these emails by choosing No Email from the drop list. If you would prefer to receive emails just not daily emails, choose Weekly Digest Email.

> **Profile Makeover: Optimization Secrets -** Daily Digest Email
>
> **LION: LinkedIn® Open Networker -** Weekly Digest Email
>
> **Human Resource Professionals -** No Email

Account

Click Account to edit this section.

Customize the updates you see on your home page

LinkedIn® by default shows quite a bit of extraneous information under All Updates on your LinkedIn® home page. People often tell me that they avoid going through their updates because of all the useless information clogging the screen. Here's some good news: There is a way to filter your updates to make your home page easier to read.

Clicking on Customize the Updates You See on Your Home Page opens a window that has a listing of different update types.

I suggest hiding:

☐ **New connections**

☐ **Group discussions and changes**

☐ **Profile changes**

☐ **Application updates**

As you become more comfortable with LinkedIn® network updates, you may decide to hide or show more updates depending on your needs.

Upgrade Your Account

I am often asked if it's worthwhile to upgrade to a premium plan. My answer is YES! When you upgrade to a premium plan, you are unlocking numerous valuable features.

Premium Badge

LinkedIn® members who pay for LinkedIn® get a premium badge that appears on their profile. This badge shows other members that you are a serious LinkedIn® user. I have repeatedly found that there is a bit of a caste system within the LinkedIn® world. There is more respect for users who pay and paying members tend to get better treatment. Looking at search results, profiles of premium members tend to congregate on the first page of results. I don't think this is a coincidence. When it comes to technical support, premium users typically receive faster response than those who do not pay. I guess the old adage is true: you do get what you pay for.

Who's Viewed Your Profile

When you upgrade and you choose to be visible, you can see almost anyone who has viewed your LinkedIn® profile over the past 90 days. This is a great way to see who's checking you out on LinkedIn®. Not only do you get to see who's viewed them, you also get to see how well your LinkedIn® profile is performing in search and keywords through graphs that chart your success and progress.

OpenLink Network

When you opt to join the OpenLink Network, you are allowing anyone on LinkedIn® to send you a message regardless of whether they are in your 1st degree network or not. The only caveat is that they too must opt in to the OpenLink Network.

Profile Organizer

The Profile Organizer allows you to save profiles and organize them into folders, where you can add notes and contact info, and see correspondence history.

This functionality delivers an almost CRM-like ability to keep track of connections and your history with them.

InMail

InMail is a way to message any LinkedIn® member outside your network, without an introduction. It's like priority mail. Unanswered InMails are credited back to your account after 7 days. InMails are not available on all premium accounts.

More Search Results

Depending on which premium account level you choose, you get access to more search results. This functionality is beneficial to those professionals using LinkedIn® for recruitment or marketing purposes.

Additional Profile Information

Lastly, you get access to additional profile information for people inside and outside your network. Basic accounts are unable to see full names of 3rd degree connections. By upgrading, you can see their full name. You also get access to expanded profile sections that include job and education details, recommendations and groups for people outside of your network.

How to Upgrade to a Premium Account

Have I convinced you that upgrading is worth it? If not, consider one more thing. Sometimes you need to get some skin in the game in order to truly commit. I have found that once my clients started paying for LinkedIn®, the more they began to use it.

Somehow, people tend to take things more seriously when they pay for it. The other aspect is it's simply the right thing to do. LinkedIn® is providing an awesome service and you will find amazing opportunities. Doesn't it make sense to support the infrastructure that allows you to network in your pajamas? By supporting LinkedIn® with a paid account, you are allowing them to collect revenue without having to resort to selling your information to marketers, like Facebook does. Let's keep LinkedIn® the product being sold by upgrading to a premium account rather than making your demographic information the product sold to marketers.

There are two places within LinkedIn® to upgrade:

- At the very top right of the LinkedIn® screen
- On the Who's Viewed My Profile page at the very bottom.

By clicking the upgrade link on the Who's Viewed My Profile page provides you with an additional, discounted LinkedIn® plan. Yes, you read that correctly. The name of the discounted plan is called The Personal Plus plan. The cost of this plan is only $7.95 per month if paid annually; otherwise it is $8.95 if paid monthly. This is a savings of $144.00 a year from the next lowest premium plan. Holy crazy savings, Batman!

If you are having difficulty finding this discounted plan, visit my Website, LinkedIn-Makeover.com. Click Free Resources on the top navigation bar for step by step video instructions.

Benchmarking Your Profile

Remember how you recorded your profile stats when you first embarked on this journey with me? Let's revisit those stats and see how well you are doing now.

Benchmarking Worksheet - AFTER

Who's Viewed Your Profile?

Your profile has been viewed by:

_____ people in the past _____ day(s).

Search Results

How many times you appeared in LinkedIn Search: _____

LinkedIn® Network Stats

_____ Connections link you to _____ professionals.

_____ New people in your Network since _____.

Improving Your Results

Are you getting more views to your LinkedIn® profile? Are you showing up more often in search? If the answer is YES! Great job! By adding the right keywords to your profile and growing your LinkedIn® network, you are getting closer to your goals and you are seeing the results. If you aren't seeing an increase in views to your profile or search results, don't worry. It takes time for your changes to take effect in LinkedIn's system. However, if more than 6 weeks has elapsed and you aren't seeing results, it's time to ask yourself some tough questions. Did you optimize for the right keywords? Remember, dynamic, problem solver, professional, and accomplished are not keywords. Are the keywords you chose skills and strengths that are in demand in today's world? You won't be found if people aren't interested in your out of date abilities. Did you upload a professionally taken profile picture? Did you spend time and really write a narrative that speaks to your reader and tells your professional story with a clear focus on your goals?

If the answer to these questions is, "Yes Donna, I did everything you told me to do!" then there is one other thing I need to mention. With LinkedIn®, it's all about using it. LinkedIn® is a huge ocean of connections and in order for you to be seen, you have to splash around. It's not enough to simply create a LinkedIn® profile and never log back in. Have you ever heard of garbage in, garbage out? You want to use LinkedIn® as a tool.

In order to be truly successful on LinkedIn®, it's important to look at it as a way to help people. Use LinkedIn® to recommend and endorse people. Use the status updates to provide links to compelling articles. Act as a connector and introduce like-minded connections. Jump into group discussions and offer advice and assistance. As soon as you start using LinkedIn® to provide value, help others, and inspire, that's when you will truly start colliding with opportunity.

In Conclusion

Your profile is now a stunning example of a powerful LinkedIn® profile. What are you waiting for? Get out there and start networking. Grab that public profile URL you created and start dropping it everywhere. Put it on your business card, link to it from your email signature, add it to your letterhead, make sure it is on your resume, get it on your sales brochures, and do not forget to link it to your other social media profiles and your Website.

Once people know you are on LinkedIn®, you will begin receiving invitations to connect. Don't just rely on other people to connect with you. Constantly expand your network by sending invitations to people you know and have recently met. Use LinkedIn® to stay in touch with people. Make your LinkedIn® contacts your new rolodex. If you use Outlook, download Outlook's toolbar to sync your LinkedIn® contacts with your Outlook contacts.

Remember to get involved in LinkedIn® Groups. Join interesting LinkedIn® Groups so you can expose yourself to new prospects and strategic partnerships. If you are looking for a job, what is your dream company? Start investigating employees of your dream company and join their LinkedIn® Groups. Start hobnobbing. Read their posts and start adding your own posts. Converse. Interact. Get your name out there.

This may be the end of the book but it doesn't have to be the end of your experience. For updates and more hints on using LinkedIn® or to hire me to optimize your profile, visit LinkedIn-Makeover.com.

LinkedIn-Makeover.com

It doesn't matter who you are or what you do, it's not easy to write about yourself.

I hear it all the time, "I can… sell snow to an Eskimo / manage complex projects / lead exceptional teams… but sell myself? NO WAY."

Besides, who can find the time to complete their LinkedIn® profile on their own?

You know this… People are Googling you. Your LinkedIn® profile is more often than not your digital introduction and first impression with the world. If your LinkedIn® profile doesn't showcase your skills and portray you as a polished professional, you are letting the ultimate opportunity just slip away.

Stop trying to figure it out on your own and hire a LinkedIn® Profile Writer to turn your LinkedIn® profile into an amazing professional portfolio that sells YOU.

We also provide training and videos on how to best leverage LinkedIn®. Get started today.

Visit LinkedIn-Makeover.com

Index

About the Author

It was back in 2009 that Donna Serdula decided it was time to save the world from poorly written LinkedIn® profiles. She founded her company Vision Board Media and the Website, LinkedIn-Makeover.com to help job seekers and employed professionals from all over the world find success on LinkedIn®.

In addition to LinkedIn® makeovers, Donna advises businesses and individuals from all over the world on executive branding, online presence, Internet marketing and social media strategies.

Donna is a noted professional public speaker. She presents on the wonders of LinkedIn®, social media, job search, and personal branding.

To continue your LinkedIn® Makeover experience visit, http://www.LinkedIn-Makeover.com

Made in the USA
San Bernardino, CA
18 October 2013